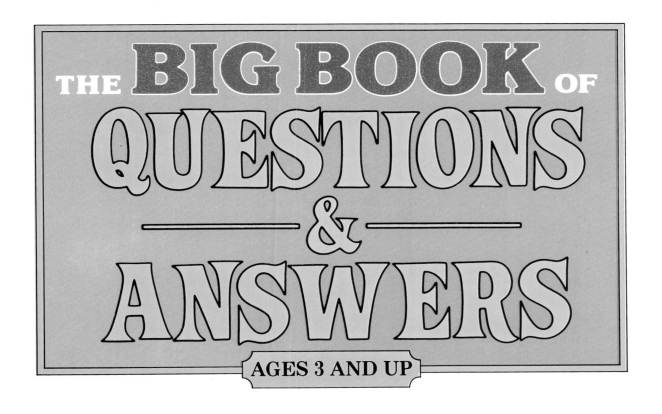

# THE BIG BOOK OF QUESTIONS & ANSWERS

AGES 3 AND UP

PUBLICATIONS INTERNATIONAL, LTD.

A. The fastest land animal is the cheetah, which can run up to 70 miles an hour.

Louis Weber, C.E.O.
Publications International, Ltd.
7373 North Cicero Avenue
Lincolnwood, Illinois 60646

Permission is never granted for commercial purposes.

Printed in Yugoslavia.

ISBN: 0-88176-670-4

Library of Congress Catalog Card Number: 89-61430

h  g  f  e  d  c  b

Contributing Authors:
Leslie Feierstone Barna
Teri Crawford Jones

Illustrated by:
T.F. Marsh
Ilene Robinette

# CONTENTS

# ANIMALS

## Q. What happens when bears hibernate?

**A.** Bears hibernate, or sleep, because there isn't enough food during the winter to eat. They choose a cave, a hollow tree, or dig a hole for a bed to sleep in. Their hearts and lungs work slowly. They do not eat or drink. They use the fat in their bodies for food.

## Q. Why do bears eat honey?

**A.** Bears love sweet-tasting things. And honey is one of the sweetest treats a bear can find. Bears can find honey by smelling. The bees make their honey from flowers. So the hive and honey smell sweet. When bears find a hive, they use their huge claws to scoop out the honey. The bear's thick fur protects it from bee stings.

## Q. Why are polar bears white?

**A.** The bear's color helps it to find food. Polar bears live in a part of the world that is usually covered with snow and ice. Often they hunt animals that have trouble seeing the bear against the white snow. The white hair also helps to trap heat from the sun.

## Q. How do bears catch fish?

**A.** Each bear catches fish in its own way. Some jump into the water. Others wait by the side of the river for fish to swim by and then grab one. One bear was seen waiting at the top of a waterfall. When the fish jumped over the rocks, the bear caught it in its mouth.

### Q. Are pandas really bears?

**A.** People who study animals spent many years trying to decide if pandas are bears. Black-and-white giant pandas look like bears, but the smaller red pandas look like raccoons. Finally, people decided that pandas really are bears.

### Q. Why are there so few pandas in the world?

**A.** Pandas usually live in places where the only food for them is bamboo plants. Sometimes the bamboo plants die or people cut down bamboo to make room for farms. Without bamboo, pandas die. Pandas do not have babies very often, so the number of pandas born does not keep up with the number of pandas that die.

### Q. Why don't people know very much about pandas?

**A.** Pandas are very shy. They hide in the bamboo. They can move quickly and quietly. People may walk right by a panda and never see it. If people cannot watch a panda, they cannot learn how it lives. Pandas in zoos do not live in the same way they do in the bamboo forest. So they do not act as they would in the wild.

**Q. Where do a cat's claws go when they are not being used?**

**A.** Cats have a claw on each toe. But you can't see the claws until they are used to scratch something. When a cat doesn't need its claws, its toes are bent. The claws are pulled back under the skin on the toes. When the cat needs its claws, the toes straighten and the claws are pulled out. If claws were always out, they would lose their sharpness when the cat walked on them.

**Q. Why does a cat like to play with yarn?**

**A.** A cat likes to chase anything that moves. If you pull a ball of yarn with little tugs, a cat might pretend it is a mouse and pounce on it. If you put a ball of yarn close to a cat's stomach, the cat might think the mouse is ready to fight. The cat will then kick the ball with its back claws. This is how many wild cats kill their food.

**Q. Why do cats have whiskers?**

**A.** Whiskers help tell cats about their world. If something like a twig touches the whiskers, cats will close their eyes to protect them. Cats will also use their whiskers to tell if there is enough room for them to fit through a tight space. Cats can even use their whiskers to tell which way the wind is blowing.

## Q. Why do tigers have stripes?

**A.** Tigers are too big and heavy to run after the animals they want to eat, so stripes help tigers hide. Tigers often hunt in long grass. The sun shining on the grass blades makes long, thin shadows that are the same shape as tigers' stripes. When tigers lie down on the grass, their dark stripes and brown fur blend with the grass and shadows. Other animals cannot see them.

## Q. Why do a tiger's eyes glow in the dark?

**A.** A tiger has special parts in the back of its eyes. These parts are like mirrors. When light shines into a tiger's eyes, the light bounces off of these parts and fills the eyeballs with light. We see this light as a glow. Because a tiger's eyes let in so much more light than people's eyes, a tiger's view of the world is fuzzier than ours. But it can see things at night that people cannot.

## Q. Do tigers like to be in water?

**A.** Tigers like water. Since they live in hot places, they often go swimming to cool off. Or they may swim to an island if they think the hunting is better there. Some people have seen tigers swim many miles.

**Q. Why is the lion called the "King of Beasts"?**

**A.** The lion is one of the largest animals in Africa. The male lion is also one of the largest of the wild cats and the only one that wears a bushy, long mane around its neck and head. People in the past thought this made the lion look like a king wearing a crown. A lion is also known to be very strong, powerful, and fearless.

**Q. What do lions do all day?**

**A.** Lions like to spend the hottest part of the day under a shady tree. The male lions may sleep up to 20 hours a day. When the sun goes down, the lions hunt for food. A male and female lion often hunt together. The male lion may chase a deer and the female lion may jump out and catch the deer as it runs by.

**Q. What kind of family does a lion have?**

**A.** Lions live in groups called *prides*. A pride has 10 to 30 lions. There is at least one male lion and several female lions. There are also young lions of different ages. Lion babies are called cubs. When they are little, cubs do nothing but play all day. But after a few months they have to learn how to hunt.

**Q. Why do squirrels store nuts for the winter?**

**A.** Squirrels gather nuts and bury them so that they will have food when snow is on the ground. Some squirrels that sleep, or hibernate, in the winter might put their nuts right by their bed so they have something to eat when they wake up. Squirrels can find buried nuts by smelling for them.

**Q. Why do many people dislike squirrels?**

**A.** Many people like to put out bird seeds for birds to eat. If there are squirrels in the neighborhood, they will knock down feeders and even chew through wire to eat the seeds. People do not like to see the birds chased away and their feeders broken. People think that squirrels are pests. Squirrels can also be a danger if they bite.

**Q. Can squirrels fly?**

**A.** There really is a flying squirrel that glides instead of flies. It has folds of skin on each side of its body attached to the front and back legs. When the squirrel stretches its legs, the skin becomes like wings, or a parachute. The squirrel can jump from a tree and glide up to 100 feet to a lower point. It uses its tail to guide its flight.

13

**Q. Why does a rabbit's nose wiggle?**

**A.** Rabbits have a good sense of smell. They are also afraid of many things. So they are always smelling the air to check for enemies. Their noses wiggle as they smell. Rabbits also move their long ears a lot to catch the sound of a possible enemy.

**Q. Why are rabbits a problem for farmers and gardeners?**

**A.** Rabbits love to eat plants. Their favorite treats are young plants that are just beginning to grow. A rabbit can ruin a farmer's field or a garden before it has a chance to grow. Rabbits also chew on the bark of fruit trees. This hurts the trees.

**Q. How fast can a rabbit hop?**

**A.** If a rabbit is running for its life, it can hop up to 30 miles an hour. This is faster than many people or dogs can run. A rabbit has very strong back legs. It uses these legs to leap far and fast. A rabbit's front legs help it to keep its balance.

### Q. Why don't people want a mouse in the house?

**A.** Mice are nice as pets in a cage. But when a wild mouse gets into a house, it causes nothing but trouble. Mice will get into cupboards and chew holes in food boxes. They will get into drawers and chew holes in clothes. They sometimes chew holes in electric cords. Mice can have many babies in a short time. So two mice in the house will soon become many.

### Q. What kind of cheese would a mouse eat?

**A.** A mouse would eat almost any kind of cheese. It is not fussy. This is probably why people put cheese in traps to catch mice. A strong-smelling cheese will attract a mouse faster. Besides cheese, grains, and vegetables, house mice have been known to eat glue, leather, and soap.

### Q. What does it mean to "play possum"?

**A.** Opossums look a little like rats. They are not very big and they do not move fast. So they have a strange way to fool enemies. If a dangerous animal comes near an opossum, the opossum will suddenly fall to the ground. It looks like it's dead. No muscles move. Even the mouth hangs open. Most animals will not eat what they haven't killed themselves. If they think the opossum is dead, they leave.

**Q. Why does a kangaroo have a pouch?**

A. A baby kangaroo crawls up and rides in its mother's pouch after it is born. The inside of the pouch is warm, furry, and dark. The little kangaroo can drink milk from its mother while it is in the pouch. After a few months, the baby is big enough to get out of the pouch and eat grass. But it will still return to the mother's pouch if it is afraid.

**Q. What is a prairie dog town like?**

A. Prairie dogs live together in large groups in burrows, or long tunnels that they dig underground. There may be many tunnels with little rooms at the end of each one. Each burrow has an entrance and an exit. The dogs enjoy spending time outside. One or more dogs always keep watch while the others look for food or play. If a watchdog hears an enemy coming, it barks a warning.

**Q. Are prairie dogs really dogs?**

A. Prairie dogs are rodents. This means they are cousins to squirrels. They got their name because they bark almost like little dogs. The bark means that there is an enemy nearby. Many prairie dogs spend time outside their homes called *burrows*. When they hear a warning bark, they run to their homes in the ground.

KANGAROO

PRAIRIE DOG

**Q. Why does a dog wag its tail?**

**A.** A dog uses its tail to talk to people and to other dogs. When a dog wags its tail, it is happy to see you and may want to play. If a dog is scared, it may put its tail between its legs. If a dog is angry, it may hold its tail in a straight line behind it.

**Q. Why do dogs pant?**

**A.** Dogs pant to help cool themselves off when they are feeling hot. They do this by hanging out their tongues to bring in cooler air. People sweat when they need to cool off, but dogs do not have the same kind of sweat glands that people do.

**Q. Why do dogs bark?**

**A.** Dogs bark to talk to people and to other dogs. Some people think that barking means dogs are upset or ready to attack. But many times dogs bark when they are asking you to play. Puppies may bark when they are lonely. Dogs also bark when they want to tell their owners about a stranger coming to the house.

**Q. Why can dogs hear dog whistles and people can't?**

**A.** Dogs have much better hearing than people do and can hear lower and higher sounds. Dog whistles give out a high-pitched sound. People will not hear the sound, but a dog will perk up its ears.

**Q. Do raccoons wash their food before eating?**

**A.** Raccoons do not really wash their food. They may dip food into water before eating it to soften the food. Raccoons have small throats. Soft food is easier for them to swallow. If a raccoon finds fruit that is already mushy, it will eat it without washing it.

**Q. What do raccoons do at night?**

**A.** Raccoons search for food at night. They are always very hungry and need lots of food. They will eat frogs and clams, fruits and berries, and nuts and grains. If people live nearby, raccoons will raid the garbage cans.

**Q. What do mother raccoons teach their babies?**

**A.** When the baby raccoons are old enough to go out at night, the mother begins teaching them. She might take them to an old tree that has fallen down to show them how to climb quickly to get away from enemies. She also shows them how to jump and hide. She teaches them how to catch grasshoppers and crickets. She may even show them how to chase a mouse.

**Q. Why don't a beaver's teeth wear out while chewing wood?**

**A.** A beaver's teeth do wear out. But their large front teeth keep growing. The front of beaver's teeth is harder than the back, so the back wears away first. This makes the beaver's teeth sharp. These are good tools for cutting wood.

**Q. What do beavers do with their tails?**

**A.** A beaver's tail is large and flat and looks like a paddle. It is used to steer the beaver in the water. It is also used to hold the beaver up while it cuts down a tree. Sometimes the tail is used to warn other beavers of danger. The beaver slaps the water with its tail. This makes a loud noise that can be heard far away.

**Q. Why do beavers build dams?**

**A.** Beavers build dams to make a small pond. In the pond, the beavers build their houses, or lodges. The dam is made of logs, branches, and rocks. Everything is held together with mud. The entrance is underwater. Inside are dry tunnels and rooms. Holes in the ceiling let in air.

**Q. Why do people think foxes are clever?**

**A.** Foxes are some of the smartest animals in the woods. To fool an enemy, foxes will often run in circles, cross streams, or walk on the top of a fence to disguise their trail. Foxes are master hunters too. They can silently sneak up on animals and pounce before the animals hear them.

**Q. What do foxes eat?**

**A.** Foxes eat anything they can catch. This includes birds, snakes, and insects. They are also fast enough to catch rabbits and squirrels. In areas that are covered with ice and snow, foxes sometimes have little to eat. So they look for leftovers of animals killed by bears and wolves. Sometimes foxes eat fruit.

**Q. Why do foxes have bushy tails?**

**A.** Foxes have bushy tails so they can run better. When foxes are running away from danger, they make quick turns. Their thick, bushy tails help them keep their balance so that they don't fall down.

**Q. Where do foxes live?**

**A.** Foxes live in *burrows* underground. They like areas that have woods, open fields, streams, and wastelands nearby. In these areas, they can find food and still be safe from people and other enemies.

### Q. Do all monkeys live in trees?

**A.** Most monkeys do live in trees. Their long arms, legs, bodies, and tails are just right for moving from branch to branch. Some monkeys, like baboons, do not live in trees. Baboons live on rocks or on the ground.

### Q. What is the difference between an ape and a monkey?

**A.** Most apes are larger than monkeys. Apes do not have tails. Almost all monkeys have tails. While there are almost 200 kinds of monkeys, there are only 4 kinds of apes. These are the chimpanzee, the gibbon, the gorilla, and the orangutan. Chimpanzees are very smart and can be trained to do many tricks.

### Q. Why do gorillas pound their chests?

**A.** Sometimes gorillas pound their chests with their hands when they are excited. When a male gorilla thinks there is danger, he will pound on his chest. He may also throw things and break branches. He hopes that he will scare away whatever threatens him. Gorillas do not pound on their chests to start fights. Gorillas are shy and gentle. Instead, they act tough.

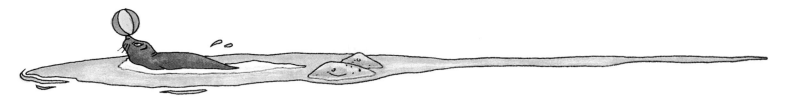

## Q. How do walruses use their tusks?

A. Walruses have two long teeth called tusks that grow down from their upper jaws. They use them to hook into ice to pull their huge bodies out of the water. They also use their husks to protect themselves against killer whales. Some walruses might use their tusks to dig clam shells from the bottom of the sea.

## Q. What are walrus herds like?

A. When walruses are not in the water, they lay on the ice in large groups. One stands guard while the others sleep. If one is in danger, others come to the rescue. Mother walruses teach their babies how to swim and find food.

## Q. How are seals and sea lions different?

A. Seals and sea lions look very much the same. But true seals do not have ear flaps on their heads. Their front flippers are also shorter than sea lions' flippers. This makes it harder for them to get around on land. But true seals can swim better because their bodies are shaped better for the water.

**Q. Why do skunks smell bad?**

**A.** Skunks usually do not smell bad. However, if they feel they are in danger, they have a secret weapon. Under their tails, skunks have two little sacs in which there is an oily liquid. They spray the liquid on an enemy. This liquid smells terrible. If it gets on the skin or in the eyes of a person or an animal, it can burn and even cause blindness.

**Q. How do skunks use their terrible smell?**

**A.** Skunks use their secret weapon as little as possible. If they think they are in danger, they will first stamp their feet and stiffen their tails. They may even growl. If this little dance doesn't work, they turn around and carefully lift their tails and spray the threatening person or animal with the liquid. The smell can last for days or even weeks. So remember to leave if you see a skunk dance.

**Q. Why are skunks black and white?**

**A.** Most animals cannot see colors the way we do. But they can see the difference between black and white. If they have been sprayed by a skunk before, they know to stay away from any animal that looks black and white. Skunks' fur comes in different patterns of black and white. They may have a wide, white stripe down their backs. Or they may be mostly black with white dots.

## Q. Why is a giraffe so tall?

**A.** A giraffe has a long neck and legs. Its neck can be over 10 feet long. A giraffe's front legs look longer than its back legs, but they are the same length. A giraffe can look over trees and spot a lion or other dangerous animals. It uses its long legs to run away. Long legs and a long neck help a giraffe find food. It can reach tree leaves that no other animals can.

## Q. Does a giraffe ever lie down?

**A.** A giraffe sleeps best when it lies down, but this is not easy for it to do. First it folds its long front legs. Next it bends its back legs. Then it bends its neck over its back. A giraffe never rolls onto its side. A giraffe is a light sleeper. It sleeps only for a few minutes at a time.

## Q. Do giraffes talk?

**A.** Giraffes are quiet animals. They rarely make a sound. This is because the voice box in their throats is not well developed. Giraffes in zoos have been heard to make a soft noise that sounds a little like a cow's moo. While they may not have much of a voice, giraffes have a wonderful sense of smell, hearing, and eyesight.

**Q. Why do camels have a hump?**

**A.** A camel's hump helps it to survive in the desert where there is little water. Before a long desert trip, a camel is given plenty of food and water. Its hump fills with fat. In the desert, the camel can live off of the fat in its hump. It does not have to eat or drink.

**Q. What do camels eat?**

**A.** Camels can go without food or water for weeks. If food is scarce, camels will eat almost anything—even leather or their owners' tents. Camels have such tough mouths that they can eat a cactus, thorns and all. People in the desert give their camels wheat, oats, dates, and grass. Zookeepers give their camels hay and grain.

**Q. How can a camel live in the desert?**

**A.** Besides a hump filled with fat, a camel's body has other things that help it live in the desert. A camel's feet are wide and thick. They will not sink in the sand. Heat, stones, and thorns will not hurt them. A camel also has small ears, thick eyelashes, and flat nostrils. These parts of a camel protect it from blowing sand.

## Q. Why is a buffalo also a bison?

**A.** When people first saw the animals that roamed the plains in the United States, they thought they looked something like the buffalo that lived in India. But people who study animals saw that the American buffalo had a larger head and neck than other buffalo. It also had humped shoulders, which other buffalo did not have. So they called this type of buffalo a bison.

## Q. What happened to all the buffalo that covered the plains?

**A.** At one time, millions of buffalo covered the American plains in large herds. The American Indians hunted the buffalo for food. When white people came, they shot thousands of buffalo for their skins and to clear the land to build a railroad. Soon there were few buffalo left. Buffalo are now protected by law.

## Q. Why do buffalo live in herds?

**A.** Buffalo like to be with other buffalo. This means they are social animals. A herd is a group of the same kind of animals that live together. Buffalo know there is safety in numbers. If danger threatens, the largest and strongest buffalo can help protect the smaller buffalo and the babies.

## Q. How did the American Indians use the buffalo?

**A.** The American Indians used buffalo for food, clothing, and shelter. The buffalo furnished excellent meat. Buffalo hide was made into clothing, tepees, shields, and boat coverings. Even the bones and horns were used.

## Q. Why do people say elephants never forget?

**A.** Elephants do forget things. But they remember what they learn better than most animals. Elephants can remember 30 or more different commands from their trainers. Elephants are also known to remember how people treat them. Even if an elephant doesn't see a person for a long time, it will remember if the person was nice or mean.

## Q. What do elephants do with their trunks?

**A.** Elephants' trunks are their noses and hands. Elephants use their trunks to smell things and to push and pull. Elephants pick up food and small things with the two fingerlike parts at the end of their trunks. They warn other elephants by trumpeting through their trunks. Elephants even give themselves baths with their trunks. They suck up the water and spray it over their backs and heads.

## Q. Are elephants really afraid of mice?

**A.** Elephants are not afraid of mice. Elephants are more likely to step on mice than run away from them. If a mouse is put in an elephant's pen, the elephant will be curious about it.

**Q. How do horses sleep?**

**A.** Horses usually sleep standing up. Their legs are made so that they lock in place to hold up the horse so it will not get tired. Horses can lie down. But because they are heavy, it takes a lot of energy for a horse to get up.

**Q. How do people use horses today?**

**A.** Before there were cars, horses were the best way to travel on land. People rode them or hooked them up to wagons. Today many people ride horses for the fun of it. Many horses are trained to compete in jumping contests and in races. Other horses are trained to put on shows. Horses also still work for people. Some horses are used to herd cattle or to plow fields.

**Q. Why do fawns have spots?**

**A.** Fawns have spots to help protect them from danger. A little fawn cannot run fast. So when the mother deer wants to eat, she tells the little fawn to lie down in long grass. The fawn lays very still and hardly breathes. Its spots blend in with the sunlight and the shadows.

**Q. Why do deer have antlers?**

**A.** In most kinds of deer, only the male has antlers. Antlers are made of bone that grows from the deer's head. Every spring the antlers grow. And every winter they fall off. A deer's antlers help it to look tall and strong. Deer can also use their antlers as weapons against enemies.

**Q. Why do pigs get dirty?**

**A.** Wild pigs living in the woods usually stay clean. Farm pigs often live in small pens where they cut up the ground and make a mess with their sharp hooves. Pigs in pens also like to roll in mud to keep cool. They can't sweat like people. Hot weather would kill them if they had no way to cool off.

**Q. Why do pigs get so fat?**

**A.** Pigs that people raise for food are special kinds of pigs that gain weight quickly. Farmers feed these pigs grain and other foods to make them grow fast. Wild pigs look a lot like tame pigs, but they are not nearly as fat. They eat what they can find and spend a lot of time running from or charging enemies. This activity burns up any fat they might have.

**Q. Are guinea pigs really pigs?**

**A.** Guinea pigs are really rodents like mice and rats. They are called pigs because they are round and sometimes fat. They squeal and grunt a little like pigs when they are hungry. But they would not like to roll in mud as a pig does. And they only eat vegetables.

GUINEA PIG

**Q. Why do birds sing?**

**A.** A bird may sing to tell other birds that a certain tree, bush, or area of land belongs to it. Male birds may sing to attract female birds. Some songs may be warnings to other birds that an enemy is nearby. Many people believe that birds sometimes sing just because they are happy.

**Q. Why do birds build nests?**

**A.** Nests are a place for birds to raise their families. Some birds build their nests in trees. Other birds build nests on the ground, on rocks, in grass by water, or even by people's houses. Nests are made of many things such as sticks, grass, leaves, and mud. When the nest is finished, the mother bird lays her eggs. When the babies hatch, the parents spend most of their time getting food for their babies.

**Q. Why can some birds talk like people?**

**A.** Parrots can imitate or sound like people talking. These birds have very good hearing. They carefully listen to sounds around them and repeat what they hear. Parrots are large birds. They have mouths and tongues large enough to form human words. Birds that repeat human words may be trying to talk to their owners as they would talk to other birds in the wild.

**Q. Why do birds have feathers instead of fur?**

**A.** Feathers are made so that they keep some air next to a bird's body. This helps keep the bird warm. Feathers are also made to help birds fly. They are smooth and light so that birds can glide through the air. When birds spread their wings, they can ride air currents. They flap their wings to go faster and higher.

**Q. Why can't an ostrich fly?**

**A.** An ostrich has wings, but the wings are too small for flying. They could never lift the ostrich's eight-foot-tall body. Instead of flying, the ostrich runs away from enemies. It has long, strong legs that help it run up to 40 miles an hour. If they cannot run, ostriches can use their legs to kick an enemy.

**Q. Does an ostrich really stick its head in the sand?**

**A.** There is an old tale that when ostriches are frightened they hide their heads in the sand. Ostriches really don't do this. But some people may have thought they did because ostriches sometimes lie down when they see an enemy. They stretch their necks along the ground so the enemy can't see them.

## Q. Why don't ducks get soaking wet?

A. Ducks spend much of their time paddling around in water. Yet they never look really wet. This is because their smooth, overlapping feathers help keep water out. The feathers also help ducks float. Ducks make a special oil that they comb through their feathers with their beaks. This oil helps water run off their bodies.

## Q. How do ducks swim?

A. Ducks have wide, webbed feet on which skin stretches between the toes. These feet can be used like paddles when the ducks are in the water. Their legs are also strong and can move their paddles quickly. Ducks' short legs and webbed feet are not so useful on land where they can only waddle.

## Q. Why does a baby duck follow its mother?

A. A baby duck must stay with its mother for safety. When a baby duck is still in its shell, it may hear its mother clucking to it. When it hatches, it knows her face and voice within a few hours. It will follow her closely when she leaves the nest. If a baby duck mixes in with other ducks, it will still know who its mother is.

**Q. Why do some fish travel in schools?**

**A.** A school is a group of fish that swim together. They may travel this way for protection. To a bigger fish, the school may look like a giant monster. All the fish in a school may be able to spot danger faster than one fish by itself. If a big fish attacks, all the swimming fish may confuse it. It wouldn't know which fish to eat first.

**Q. Why do fish have fins?**

**A.** Fish have fins instead of legs. They use their fins like paddles to push them through the water. By swaying their bodies back and forth, the fish move their fins. Fish also use their fins to stay upright in the water. Without fins, the fish might just roll over.

**Q. Do fish talk?**

**A.** For a long time, people didn't think fish made any noise. No one had heard them. But people now have machines that can hear sounds underwater. They put the machines in the ocean. The people heard all kinds of noises—thumps, clicks, grunts, and calls. They figured out that these noises were fish talking. A fish called a croaker sounds like a bullfrog. You can imagine what a school of croakers would sound like!

DOLPHIN

**Q. What are dolphins and porpoises?**

**A.** Dolphins and porpoises are small whales. They are a part of a group of whales that have teeth. Most of them live in the ocean. Like all whales, they breathe air and have blowholes on the top of their bodies. Dolphins are larger than porpoises and have a more pointed nose. Their upturned mouths look like smiles. Dolphins' noses are called beaks.

**Q. Do dolphins talk?**

**A.** Dolphins are one of the smartest animals on earth. Many people believe dolphins have a language of their own. Dolphins have been heard talking to each other with many kinds of sounds. They make high whistles, clicks, and barks. Each sound means something different. Some dolphins have even learned to repeat human words.

**Q. Which sharks are dangerous?**

**A.** More than 300 kinds of sharks swim in the ocean. Only a few are dangerous to people. These include the great white shark, the blue shark, tiger shark, hammerhead, and the gray nurse shark. Meat-eating sharks usually eat fish. They are hungry most of the time. So they spend their days looking for food.

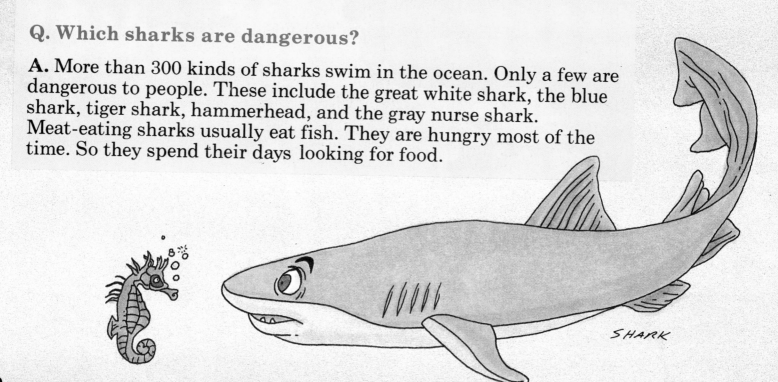

SHARK

## Q. How big can whales get?

**A.** The largest animal that has ever lived on earth is the blue whale. It can weigh up to 140 tons and grow to 98 feet long. This is about what 18 large elephants weigh all together.

## Q. How do whales breathe?

**A.** Whales live in the ocean. But they breathe air just like people do. Whales have huge lungs. They can also store air throughout their chests. The air they breathe in can last them for up to two hours underwater. When the whale comes up for air, it spouts out the used air through a blowhole on the top of its head.

## Q. What do whales eat?

**A.** Many whales live on the tiniest animals in the ocean. When the whale sees a mass of shrimp and sea plants, it swims forward and opens its mouth. After the mouth closes, the tongue pushes the water out. A row of thin bones attached to the whale's jaw traps the food like a comb. Then the whale swallows.

## Q. Do whales play?

**A.** Whales have been seen jumping out of the water and swimming around as though they were playing. Sometimes whales will dive under a bunch of seaweed. When they come up, the whales are wearing seaweed on their heads. The seaweed moves down to the whales' tails as they swim. Then they flip it forward and bat it with their front flippers.

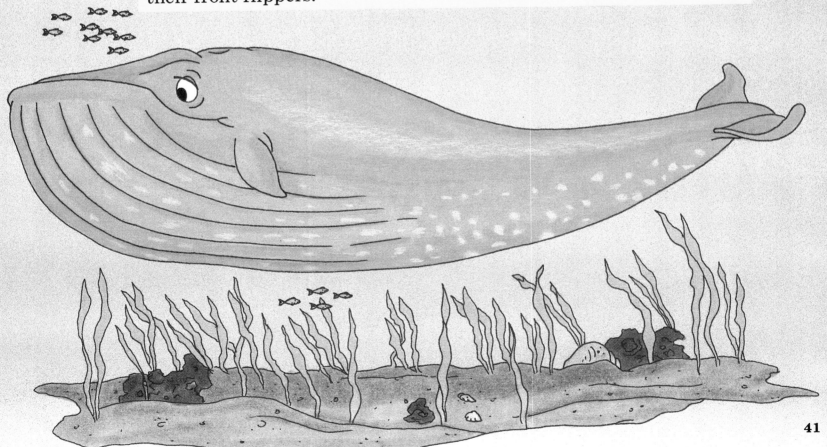

## Q. What is the difference between frogs and toads?

**A.** Toads and frogs are very much alike. However, a frog has a smooth, wet-feeling skin and long hind legs. A toad has a rougher, bumpy skin and short legs. Although these bumps look like warts, they are really little sacks that have a liquid in them. Any animal that tries to eat a toad will not like the taste of this liquid.

## Q. What are tadpoles?

**A.** Tadpoles are baby frogs. However, they look more like fish. They just have heads and tails. After five weeks, the tadpoles begin to grow legs. Inside their bodies their lungs begin to grow. After ten weeks, the front legs grow. The tail disappears. Now the tadpole looks like a frog. It will be able to leave the water when it is three months old.

## Q. How do frogs catch flies?

**A.** Frogs catch flies with their tongues. A frog's mouth is wide and its tongue is long and sticky. When a frog sees a tasty fly, it opens its mouth and shoots out its tongue. The fly sticks to the tongue. A frog can also catch other tasty meals such as small fish, worms, and spiders with its quick tongue.

## Q. How do frogs make a croaking sound?

**A.** A male frog croaks in order to attract a female frog. He breathes in air, closes his nostrils and mouth, and forces the air back and forth between his mouth and lungs. As the air passes over his vocal cords, it causes them to vibrate and make a croaking sound.

FROG

TOAD

**Q. Why do turtles have a shell?**

**A.** Turtles move slowly. They cannot run away from their enemies. So they need hard shells. When another animal attacks a turtle, it pulls in all the soft parts of its body. The turtle waits while the animal tries to bite the hard shell. Finally, the animal gives up and leaves. Slowly, the turtle comes out of its shell and goes on its way.

**Q. How do turtles get their heads and legs into their shell?**

**A.** Many turtles have thin necks. When the turtle stretches its neck out, the bones in its neck move apart. When the turtle pulls its neck in, the bones move together. Some long-necked turtles have to bend their necks to get their heads in their shells. The turtle uses the same kind of movement to pull in its legs.

**Q. Can a turtle get out of its shell?**

**A.** When a turtle is turned over on its back, it probably wishes it could get out of its shell. Once a turtle is turned over, it is helpless. But a turtle cannot get out of its shell. The shell is a part of its body. In fact, the shell grows from a turtle's ribs. Without its shell a turtle will die.

**Q. Why does a snake's tongue dart in and out?**

**A.** A snake uses its tongue like people use their noses. When a snake flicks its tongue, it picks up bits of things that all animals, plants, and things give off. Its tongue brings the bits into the snake's mouth. The top of its mouth has a special part that can smell the bits. The snake then learns a lot about what is around it.

**Q. How does a snake eat things bigger than its head?**

**A.** A snake has a small head and a very big mouth. This is because the snake's jaw bones are loose. They can open very wide. The snake stretches its mouth over its dinner. Its jaws and sharp teeth pull the food into its throat. The snake's stretchy skin expands to let the food go down the throat. The meal may be an egg, a mouse, a frog, or even a rabbit.

**Q. How does a snake move without legs?**

**A.** Inside a snake's body is one long backbone made up of many smaller bones and ribs. When the snake moves, its muscles bend and move this long line of bones. That is why a snake seems to ripple as it moves. A snake cannot move on a smooth surface. It needs a rough surface against which to push its body. A snake cannot move in a straight line. Its body moves along the ground in curves.

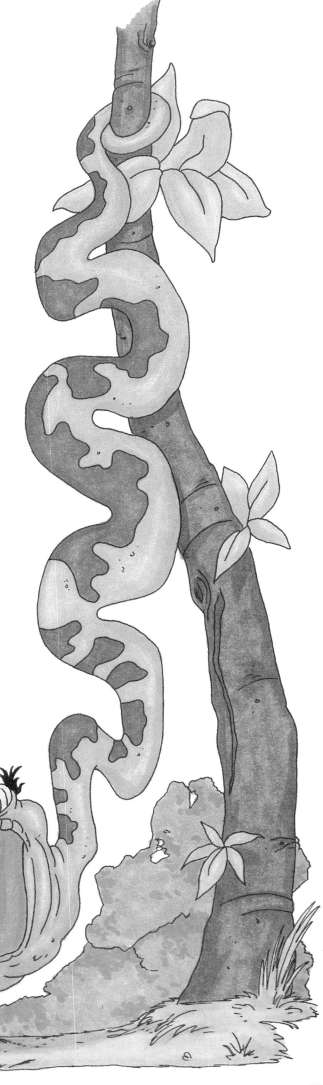

CROCODILE

OTTER

ALLIGATOR

### Q. How are crocodiles and alligators different?

**A.** Crocodiles and alligators are both reptiles. They also look much the same. But a crocodile's nose is pointed. An alligator's nose is rounded. The crocodile is also smaller than an alligator and can move more quickly.

### Q. Why do otters play?

**A.** Otters are long, furry animals that look like weasels. They live near rivers, streams, and oceans. When otters are little, they enjoy wrestling and chasing each other. Sometimes they will slide down a mud bank into the water over and over again. The games that little otters play teach them how to hunt and live in their world.

### Q. How do otters eat?

**A.** Many otters swim after a fish and catch it with their handlike paws. They take the fish to shore and hold it down to eat. Sea otters like to eat fish that live in shells. The otter sometimes holds a shell on its stomach in the water. Then it hits the shell with a rock to break it. The otter uses its stomach as a dinner table.

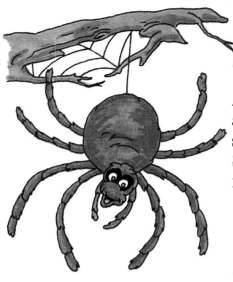

### Q. Are spiders bugs?

**A.** Spiders are not bugs. They're not even insects. They are a part of a group of animals called arachnids. Their cousins are ticks and scorpions. All arachnids have eight legs. Insects have six legs. Spiders help people by cleaning their houses of flies, moths, and mosquitoes. But they add their own mess by making cobwebs.

### Q. Why do spiders spin webs?

**A.** Spiders spin webs to catch insects for food. They make their webs from a liquid silk in their bodies. They coat some of the thin threads with sticky stuff. This stuff can trap insects much larger than the spider. When the spider feels a tug on the web, it runs out and spins threads around the insect to make sure it doesn't get away.

### Q. Where do butterflies come from?

**A.** Butterflies have four parts to their lives. They hatch from tiny eggs. Then they are little, wormlike animals called caterpillars. They spend their days eating plants and growing. One day caterpillars stop eating. They make a silk thread from their bodies and wrap it completely around themselves. This hardens and becomes a cocoon. Inside the butterfly begins to form. After many weeks, the new butterfly breaks free. When its wings dry, it can fly.

# NATURE

## Q. Why does the sun shine?

**A.** The sun is made of very hot gases. What we call sunshine are these very hot gases burning. Imagine how hot they are if they give the earth heat and light when we are so far away.

## Q. Why doesn't the sun shine at night?

**A.** Each day the earth spins around one time. As the earth spins, one side of it faces the sun. On that side of the earth it is daytime. On the side that faces away from the sun it is nighttime. The sun is always shining, but when the side of the earth on which you live spins away from the sun, you cannot see it.

## Q. What does gravity do?

**A.** The earth pulls everything that is on it or near it. This pull is called *gravity*. Each person on earth is pulled as much as he or she weighs. The gravity of the moon is only one-sixth as strong as the gravity on the earth. So if you weigh 42 pounds on earth, you would only weigh 7 pounds on the moon.

## Q. Why do people float in outer space?

**A.** When people are in outer space they are far enough from the earth that no gravity pulls them. If they are half-way between the earth and the moon, gravity from neither pulls them and they really have no weight.

**Q. How big is the moon?**

**A.** To us on earth, the moon seems to be much bigger than any of the stars in the sky. That is because it is our nearest neighbor. The moon is very small compared with the earth. It would take about 4 moons together to make up the size of the earth.

**Q. Why does the moon shine?**

**A.** The moon does not have light of its own like the sun. But it can send back some of the light that shines on it from the sun. That is why we can see the moon in the sky.

**Q. Why doesn't the moon always look round?**

**A.** One part of the moon is always facing the sun. The other side of the moon is dark. We can only see the part of the moon that is lit by the sun. Since different amounts of the moon are lit by the sun on different nights, sometimes we see a whole circle and sometimes we see just a small piece.

**Q. Is there really a "man in the moon"?**

**A.** When people look at the moon at night, they sometimes think they see a man's face. What they are really seeing are deep holes called *craters* and mountains that are on the moon's surface. No one lives on the moon.

**Q. Why do stars twinkle?**

**A.** Stars seem to twinkle when we look at them from the earth. This happens because a star's light passes through the air that is all around the earth before it reaches our eyes. When a star's light passes through this air, the star looks as if it is twinkling.

**Q. How many stars are in the sky?**

**A.** If you tried to count the stars on a very clear night, away from the lights of cities and towns, you might reach about 3,000. With the help of very powerful telescopes, many more stars can be seen. There are millions and millions of stars in the universe.

**Q. Why are there star pictures in the sky?**

**A.** People have been studying the stars for thousands of years. Some people thought that if you connected the stars like you connect the dots in a dot picture you could draw a make-believe picture. These make-believe star pictures are called *constellations*.

**Q. What are the names of the planets?**

**A.** Our sun is really a big star. There are 9 planets that circle around the sun. Their names are Mercury, Venus, Earth, Mars, Jupiter, Saturn, Uranus, Neptune, and Pluto. Earth is the third-closest planet to the sun.

**Q. Can we see the other planets?**

**A.** We can see some of the planets. But some are so far away from the earth, they can only be seen with a telescope. You can tell when you are looking at a planet because it shines with a bright, steady light. Planets usually don't twinkle like stars.

**Q. Do people live on any of the planets?**

**A.** The only planet where people can live is the earth. The other planets do not have air to breathe. It is also much too hot or too cold on other planets for people.

## Q. Why are there clouds in the sky?

**A.** Clouds are made up of tiny droplets of water. There are always tiny drops of water in the air, but you cannot see them. But when many droplets are pushed together, a cloud is made. When this happens, what you see is water.

## Q. Are there different kinds of clouds?

**A.** All clouds are made of the same tiny droplets of water. But there are different kinds of clouds. Some clouds are big and puffy and you see them on days when there is lots of sunshine. Other clouds are very high up in the sky and look feathery. Still other clouds are thick and dark. They are the clouds that bring rain.

## Q. What makes fog?

**A.** Fog is made of water droplets just like clouds. Fog is a cloud that is on the ground instead of in the sky. You can see a cloud of fog all around you. Fog makes it hard to see where you are going.

## Q. Why are there shadows?

**A.** When a person or a thing blocks light, a shadow appears. The sun can shine on you and around you, but not through you. When your body blocks the light, your shadow appears!

## Q. Why does the size of a shadow change?

**A.** The sun is low in the sky in the early morning and late afternoon. At these times of day, your shadow is long and skinny. When the sun is high overhead, your shadow is short and fat.

## Q. Where does shade come from?

**A.** Shade is a very large shadow. For instance, a very big tree will make a very big shadow. Shade is what we call the shadow under the tree.

## Q. Can groundhogs really predict the weather?

**A.** Groundhogs are believed to predict the weather by coming out of hibernation on February 2, which is called "Groundhog Day." If a groundhog comes out of its burrow and sees its shadow on a clear day, this is a bad sign. The groundhog goes back to its burrow to get six more weeks of sleep. If the day is cloudy and the groundhog can't see its shadow, it stays outside. This is a good sign. It means the weather will be mild for the rest of the winter. But this idea that the groundhog can predict the weather is not really true. It is just a story people made up.

**Q. Why is there air?**

**A.** Air is a mixture of many different gases. It extends for many miles above the earth's surface. Because the earth has gravity, it pulls the air close to itself. It is very important to have air on the earth because all living things need it to live.

**Q. Why is the sky blue?**

**A.** The gases that are in the air are what make the sky look blue. Light from the sun shines through the gases in the air. There are different colors of light. Blue light is the color we see as the sun shines through the air. That is why the sky looks blue.

**Q. Why does the sky look so colorful at sunset?**

**A.** Some colors of light are very long and others are very short. When the sun sets in the evening, the long colors of light bounce off the gases in the air. These long colors are red, pink, and orange.

**Q. Why does the wind blow?**

**A.** Light from the sun warms the air that is all around the earth. When air is heated it begins to move. The warmer air gets, the faster it begins to move. Another name for moving air is wind.

**Q. How can the wind help people?**

**A.** When you think of the wind, you probably think of strong winds or windstorms. But the wind can also help people. Winds can give things power. A windmill needs the power of the wind in order to work. Sailboats need the wind in order to go. And kites need wind in order to fly.

**Q. Why is there snow?**

**A.** Snow is really frozen rain. Droplets of water that are in a cloud form tiny ice crystals that turn into snowflakes. Snow is made of water and air. In fact, snow is mostly air. This means that a very small amount of water will make a large amount of snow.

**Q. Where do snowflakes come from?**

**A.** Snowflakes are formed from tiny crystals of frozen water droplets. As the flakes grow, they take on different shapes. Different kinds of flakes make different kinds of snow. The kind of flakes that grow when water droplets freeze depends on what the temperature is. Very cold air makes very light, dry snow. The warmer the air, the wetter the snow.

## Q. Why does it rain?

**A.** When a cloud gets very big, the small droplets of water that it is made up of begin to bump into each other. This makes them join together to form big drops. The big drops are so heavy that they cannot float in the air. So they fall to earth as rain.

## Q. Where does a rainbow come from?

**A.** Sometimes at the end of a rain shower the sun shines through the clouds. The tiny drops of water that are still in the air break the sunlight into the beautiful colors of a rainbow. Some people think that rainbows are lucky. But, as yet, no one has ever found a pot of gold at the end of a rainbow!

## Q. Can thunder and lightning hurt you?

**A.** Only lightning can hurt you. Thunder is just air shaking very hard. A flash of lightning is really a big flash of electricity that we can see from very far away. Electricity is very hot. Lightning can burn whatever it touches.

## Q. What makes thunderstorms?

**A.** Thunderstorms are caused by *thunderheads*, which are big, fluffy clouds. They build up on very hot, humid days when the warm air on the ground heats up the moist air above it and makes it rise very fast. Little drops of water gather into the big clouds and cool the air very quickly. The cool air sinks to a lower part of the thunderhead. There, the air warms up again and rises. The rising and falling air makes very strong winds in the cloud. Large raindrops fall and you can see lightning and hear thunder.

**Q. What is hail made of?**

A. Hail is really frozen rain. It forms when whole raindrops freeze as they fall throught the thin, cold air in the sky. Hailstones are thicker than snowflakes. They do not melt as quickly. That is why hail can fall in the summertime. Hailstones can weigh as much as 2 pounds! You can imagine the damage that a 2-pound hailstone can do.

**Q. What happens during a hurricane?**

A. Hurricanes are rainstorms that have very strong winds. They begin over the ocean. Sometimes hurricanes move closer to land. When this happens, very heavy rains fall and the winds begin to blow. Hurricanes can cause a lot of damage.

**Q. What are tornadoes?**

A. Tornadoes are storms that are even stronger than hurricanes. They begin over land as a tall column of air that looks like a funnel. They also cause a lot of damage. But a tornado can only do damage to things that are directly in its path.

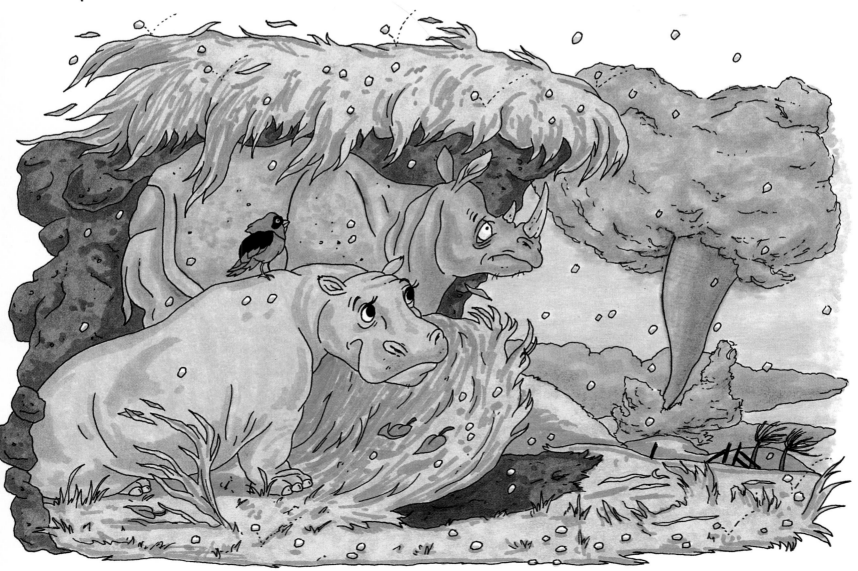

**Q. Why can you see your breath in the air when it is cold outside?**

**A.** Your breath has very tiny droplets of water in it. Since it is warm inside your mouth, your breath is warm. When you blow out a breath of warm, wet air, it looks like a small cloud when it touches the cold air.

**Q. Who is Jack Frost?**

**A.** Have you ever awakened on a very cold morning and found beautiful patterns of ice on the windows? What a pretty surprise! People sometimes say that it was Jack Frost who made the icy patterns on the window. Jack Frost does not really exist.

**Q. Is there really a North Pole?**

**A.** Yes, there really is a North Pole. But there isn't really a pole sticking in the snow that says "North Pole." The North Pole is the name of a place at the very top of the earth.

**Q. Why do plants have roots?**

**A.** Plants use their roots like a bug uses its feelers. The tips of a plant's roots push into the dirt looking for water and other things that the plant needs to make food. Did you know that sometimes a plant's roots are bigger than the plant you see above the ground?

**Q. Why do trees have bark?**

**A.** A tree's bark is a covering that protects the wood inside. Bark keeps the tree from losing too much water. Bark also keeps insects and other pests from eating the wood. You can think of a tree's bark as its coat. This coat keeps the tree from getting too cold or too hot.

**Q. How can you tell how old a tree is?**

**A.** If you look at the stump of a tree, you will see rings of different-colored wood. By counting the rings, you can tell how many years old the tree is. Trees have rings because a new layer of wood grows under the bark each year. When a tree trunk is cut, the layers of wood look like rings.

**Q. Why do trees lose their leaves in autumn?**

**A.** Trees lose a lot of water through their leaves. In winter, when the soil freezes, a tree's roots have a hard time finding enough water. Trees shed their leaves in the fall to save water during the cold winter months.

**Q. How do trees know when to shed their leaves?**

**A.** As the summer months go by, the days begin to get shorter and shorter as fall begins. Along with the days becoming shorter, the air begins to get cooler. When there is more darkness and cooler weather, a tree gets the signal that it is time to shed its leaves.

**Q. How do a tree's leaves change color?**

**A.** When a tree gets ready to shed its leaves, it seals the stems of the leaves off from the branches. The leaves cannot get water to make food. As they begin to die, they slowly lose their green color. As the green color fades, the leaves turn yellow, orange, red, or brown.

**Q. Why are plants green?**

**A.** Plants can make their own food. To help them do this, they have a green substance in them called *chlorophyll*. It is chlorophyll that gives plants their green color.

**Q. How many kinds of plants are there?**

**A.** There are plants living in almost every part of the earth. Plants can live on land, under the sea, in deserts, on rocks, and even inside of animals. Some of the tiniest of all living things are plants. The largest of all living things is also a plant. Scientists guess that there are about 350,000 different kinds of plants in the world.

**Q. Why do plants need water?**

**A.** If a plant does not get enough water, it will die. A plant loses water through its leaves. In order to have enough water, a plant needs to have a constant supply so it can take in more water from its roots. Water is needed so that a plant can make food.

**Q. Does a plant feel pain when you cut it?**

**A.** Animals feel pain because they have nerve cells that can carry messages of pain to their brains. Plants have neither brains nor nerve cells. So a plant cannot feel pain the way people and animals can.

**Q. Does talking to a plant make it grow better?**

**A.** Scientists are not really sure whether talking to plants helps them grow. Some scientists think that sounds do have some effect on plants. They think that soft, pretty music helps them to grow. They also think that loud, harsh music can have a bad effect on plants.

**Q. What things that people use come from plants?**

**A.** The furniture in your home comes from plants. The wood it is made out of comes from trees. Rubber things are made from the sap of rubber trees. Many kinds of cloth such as cotton come from plants. Many medicines are also made from plants.

## Q. Why are there flowers?

**A.** Flowers have seeds inside them that grow into new plants. A flower's brightly colored petals attract insects and other animals. These insects and animals help to scatter the seeds so that new plants could grow.

## Q. Why do some flowers smell sweet?

**A.** Just as flowers have colors to make animals come to them, they also smell sweet. The sweet smell of some flowers also causes bees, birds, and bugs to come to the flower to help spread seeds.

## Q. Why can some flowers bloom in the snow?

**A.** Sometimes you can see small flowers poking through the ground even when there is snow. Over time, these flowers have grown and changed little by little until they can live even in very cold weather.

## Q. Why are 4-leaf clovers supposed to be lucky?

**A.** Hundreds of years ago, people thought that ordinary 3-leaf clovers were lucky. Since 4-leaf clovers are very rare, people thought that they were even luckier. It is only superstition to think that 4-leaf clovers bring good luck.

## Q. What are clovers used for?

**A.** Even though it is only superstition to think that clovers are lucky, clovers can be thought of as good plants. They add good nutrients to the soil. Many useful farm animals such as cows eat clovers. Bees like clovers, and some of the best honey is made from clovers.

**Q. Where does dirt come from?**

**A.** Dirt is mostly made of very tiny pieces of rock. Tiny pieces of clay and sand and tiny droplets of water are also in dirt. Many living things such as worms and bugs make their home in dirt too.

**Q. How was dirt made?**

**A.** Millions of years ago, there was no dirt on the earth. There were only very large rocks and water. Rain and wind beat against the rocks. Oceans and rivers pounded against the rocks. Slowly, the rocks were worn down into small rocks, stones, and pebbles. Pieces of dead plants and animals were mixed in with the tiny rocks. This mixture that formed was dirt.

**Q. Why do weeds grow?**

**A.** Weeds are plants that grow where people don't want them to grow. If you are growing a garden filled with beautiful flowers, you would work very hard to pull out all the weeds. You wouldn't want the weeds to use the water and food that the flowers need.

**Q. Are weeds always bad?**

**A.** Since weeds usually grow where people don't want them to, most people think of weeds as bad. But weeds are good for some things. Some weeds have very pretty flowers. Certain weeds can be made into medicines, dyes, and other things that people use. People even eat some weeds—dandelion leaves are sometimes put in salads.

**Q. Why are some plants poisonous?**

**A.** Scientists think that some plants have poison to protect themselves from being eaten by animals. Other scientists think that plants with poisons grew by accident because not all poisonous plants harm animals.

**Q. What makes a plant poisonous?**

**A.** A plant is thought to be poisonous if it does harm to an animal that either eats or touches it. Not all plant poisons act in the same way. Some poisons affect the nerves. Some keep the heart from beating properly. Other poisons can hurt the skin and cause itchy rashes. Poison ivy is one poisonous plant you may know.

**Q. What is a forest made of?**

**A.** Forests are big areas of land that are usually covered with trees. Many different kinds of creatures live in forests. Some of the creatures are tiny. Others are among the largest of all living things. They all depend on each other to survive.

## Q. Why can water boil?

**A.** When water gets very hot, the tiny parts that make up water begin to move faster and faster. When they get really hot, they begin to turn into a gas. This gas is steam. The steam rises from the boiling water and goes into the air.

## Q. Why does water freeze?

**A.** As water cools, the tiny parts of water begin to move very slowly. The colder it gets, the slower they move. The tiny droplets begin to move closer and closer together until they get hard. When they get really hard they turn to ice.

## Q. Why do wet things shine?

**A.** Things that are very smooth look shiny. This is because light bounces off smooth things. This does not happen with things that are rough. However, when rough things get wet, water fills in the tiny holes on the surface making them look smooth. This is why even rough things look shiny when they are wet.

## Q. Why is ice slippery?

**A.** If you try to hold a piece of ice, it usually slips out of your hand. The warmness of your fingers causes the ice to melt. When this happens, a thin layer of water comes between your fingers and the ice. This is what makes the ice feel slippery.

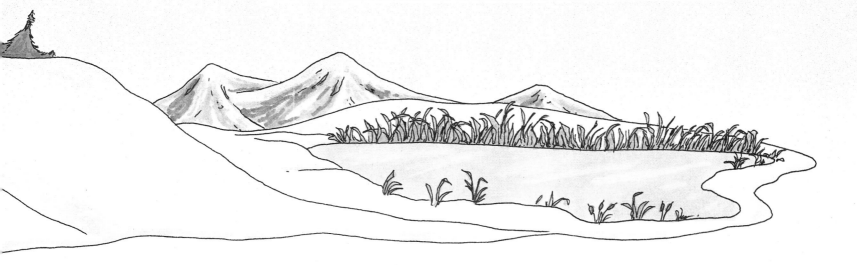

**Q. What is the difference between a lake and a pond?**

**A.** Some people say that a pond is more shallow than a lake. They call a body of water a pond when it is shallow enough for sunlight to reach its bottom. But some lakes are shallow too. Scientists usually agree that lakes, no matter how deep or shallow they are, are always bigger than ponds.

**Q. Why are there waterfalls?**

**A.** A waterfall is made when there is a change in the height of a river. Water flowing down a river must fall when the land under the river becomes lower all of a sudden. The water has nowhere to go but down.

**Q. Can a waterfall ever stop?**

**A.** Believe it or not, every waterfall will stop someday. It may take a very long time— sometimes hundreds or thousands of years. When enough time passes, the falling water will smooth down the rocks it passes over, and there will be no need for the water to fall.

**Q. What is the biggest ocean in the world?**

**A.** The Pacific Ocean is the largest ocean in the world. It is larger than the Atlantic Ocean and the Indian Ocean put together! At its widest point, the Pacific Ocean reaches almost halfway around the world.

**Q. Why are there waves?**

**A.** Waves form way out at sea as winds blow. The wind pushes small drops of water and they start to move around very quickly. Near land the sea is shallow. The ocean floor stops the water from moving, and waves break onto the shore.

**Q. Why is sea water salty?**

**A.** There are many different minerals in sea water. These minerals came from the land and were washed into the sea by moving rivers. Of all the minerals in the sea, salt is present in the largest amount.

**Q. Where do tides come from?**

**A.** If you ever sat on the beach and watched the ocean water as it came closer and closer, you were watching the tide come in. Perhaps you also saw the water move farther and farther away later in the day. More and more beach showed as the tide went out. Tides are caused by the pull of the moon's gravity. It tugs at the oceans' water.

**Q. How do rivers form?**

**A.** A river is usually part of a number of smaller streams. This is called a *river system*. A very tiny stream called a *rivulet* usually flows into a larger stream. This larger stream will be joined by other streams. Finally, all of the streams will join into a river.

**Q. Where do rivers get their water?**

**A.** River water comes in part from rainwater that flows along the ground. It also comes from melting snow and ice. Some water in rivers even comes from lakes and natural openings in the ground called *springs*.

**Q. Where do icebergs come from?**

**A.** Icebergs are large mountains of ice that float in the sea. Icebergs form in places that are very cold. They begin to float to warmer areas, and little by little, they start to melt.

**Q. Why are icebergs dangerous?**

**A.** The part of an iceberg that you can see is really only the tip. Most of the iceberg is hidden under the sea. You can imagine how dangerous an iceberg is for a ship that is sailing near it.

**Q. Why are there mountains?**

**A.** Most mountains are made from rock that was pushed up from the bottom of the oceans. This process took many thousands of years. Other mountains were formed along cracks in the earth's surface. The land on either side of the crack was pushed up or down and formed mountains.

**Q. How big is a mountaintop?**

**A.** The tops of some mountains are so small and pointed that there is hardly enough room for a person to stand on them. Other mountains have tops that are very large. They are so large that you and many of your friends can play baseball on them. Some are even larger.

**Q. Why is there snow on top of a mountain?**

**A.** There is snow on top of very tall mountains even in summertime. This happens because the air at the top of mountains is very thin. This thin air gets very cold and the snow never melts.

**Q. Why do volcanoes erupt?**

**A.** When a volcano erupts, melted rock or lava comes out from the center of the earth. Some of the lava comes out when a volcano erupts. But some is stored in a place deep inside the volcano. When hot gases inside the earth push the lava out, the volcano erupts again.

**Q. What are rocks made of?**

**A.** Rocks are made of minerals. These are the speckles you see when you look at a rock carefully. Minerals have different colors and shapes. By looking at the minerals in a rock, scientists can tell what kind of rock it is.

**Q. How old are rocks?**

**A.** The oldest rocks that scientists know of are about 3.8 billion years old. This is the same age as the earth. The oldest of all rocks can be found on the moon. Space rocks that have landed on earth are also very old.

**Q. Why do diamonds sparkle?**

**A.** The diamonds that we see in jewelry have been cut and polished. Diamonds are cut in a special way. This special method makes many smooth surfaces on the diamond. Light bounces off of these surfaces. That is why if you hold up a diamond to the light it sparkles and shines.

**Q. What are deserts like?**

**A.** Deserts are large areas of land that are very dry. They are very dry because very little rain falls. Even though there is mostly sand on a desert, many different things can live there.

**Q. Are deserts always hot?**

**A.** During the day, the temperature in a desert gets very hot. There are no clouds in the sky and no shade. So the sun burns down and heats the land all day. But at night when the sun goes down, a desert can get very cold.

**Q. Are there storms on a desert?**

**A.** Even in a very dry desert, *some* rain falls. Once in a while, there can be a heavy rainstorm. Sometimes these rainstorms cause floods. There can also be storms in a desert without rain. Very strong winds blow across the desert whipping up sand and dust. Sandstorms can last for many days at a time.

**Q. How big was the biggest dinosaur?**

**A.** The *brontosaurus* was one of the biggest of all dinosaurs. It was about 70 feet long. Scientists think that it weighed about 30 tons. That's as big as 10 elephants! Another huge dinosaur was the *brachiosaurus*. This dinosaur was about 40 feet tall and may have weighed as much as 80 tons. It is possible that there were even bigger dinosaurs.

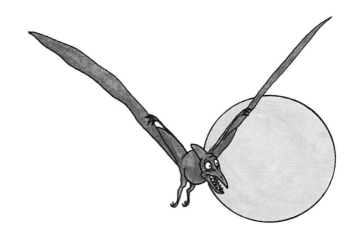

**Q. Why aren't there any dinosaurs today?**

**A.** Scientists don't really know why there are no dinosaurs today. One reason may be that the earth became colder and the plants and animals that the dinosaurs ate died. When a dinosaur had nothing to eat it died too.

**Q. Where do caves come from?**

**A.** Caves are made from soft rock. For many thousands of years, rainwater dripped down through small holes in the rock. Slowly, the rock was worn down, and a hollow cave was formed.

**Q. What are the "icicles" inside of caves?**

**A.** In some caves, water runs along the ceiling. As it drips down to the cave floor, it carries with it some of the minerals from the rock. Over time, the water escapes into the air. But the minerals do not. The minerals are left behind and form what look like stone icicles.

# FOOD

### Q. Where does food come from?

**A.** Food is grown on farms around the world. It comes from the ground. It is picked from trees. It is taken from the oceans. People are lucky that they are able to eat many different things. A lot of food is put in cans or packages. Then it is taken to your neighborhood store where people can buy it.

### Q. Why do people eat food?

**A.** Food is what you eat to stay alive. Food is the bread, vegetables, and fruit you eat. It is also the milk you drink. Children especially need food to help them grow and be healthy. Some foods are good for your body. Other foods are not as good. It's important to learn what food is best to eat.

### Q. Why do different families eat different food?

**A.** There are more ways to make things to eat than you can ever imagine. You may find that a friend's family has favorite foods you've never tasted. Different countries have their own ways of cooking food. People learn about food from their parents and grandparents.

**Q. What is bread made of?**

**A.** The main part of bread is a powdery stuff called flour. Flour is made from the seeds of plants called *grains*. There are six main kinds of grains that people grow to eat. They are wheat, corn, rice, oats, rye, and barley. To make bread, the flour is mixed with water, salt, milk, and oil. Then it is baked.

**Q. Why do people eat cereal for breakfast?**

**A.** In the morning, many people are in a hurry to get to work, school, or outside to play. Cereal is quick and easy. You just pour it in a bowl, put milk on it, and eat it. Cereal also tastes good and is good for you.

**Q. Why does some cereal float?**

**A.** When some cereals are made, they are puffed with air. This makes them very light so they float in milk. The cereals that float the best are also toasted so they are crunchy on the outside. Then the milk can't get into the cereal as easily to make it soggy.

**Q. Where does the milk in the store come from?**

**A.** Most of the milk we drink in the United States comes from cows. Farmers milk cows twice a day with milking machines. First the milk is put into large, clean glass jars. Then it goes into a big tank that chills the milk to keep it fresh. At the milk factory, the milk is put in cartons and delivered to the stores.

**Q. Does all milk come from cows?**

**A.** No. Some people drink goat's milk. In countries where there are no cows, people get their milk from such animals as reindeer, camels, or water buffalo. There is a even a special milk that is made from a plant called soybeans.

**Q. What kinds of birds do people eat?**

**A.** You may be most familiar with the bird that is often served on Christmas and Thanksgiving. That bird is turkey. Some people also like to have goose for Christmas. A goose is large like a turkey. Other birds that people eat are chicken, duck, game hens (a small chicken), and pheasant. You might even see dove, pigeon, or partridge on some dinner tables.

**Q. Do people eat any eggs besides chicken eggs?**

**A.** In the United States, people eat chicken eggs. In other parts of the world, however, people eat different bird eggs, such as duck, quail, and ostrich.

**Q. What are vegetables?**

**A.** Vegetables are all the stems, leaves, roots, seeds, or flowers of a plant. The roots we eat are brown, yellow, or red. They include potatoes, beets, and carrots. The leaf vegetables are green. These include lettuce and spinach. Peas are seeds. Celery is a stem. Broccoli is flowers and stems. Vegetables have so many good things in them, it's important to eat some of them every day.

**Q. Why are corn cobs called "ears of corn"?**

**A.** A corn plant is tall with long, green leaves that grow up and then droop down. The corn cobs grow up and to the side of the stalk, next to the leaves. People once thought that they looked like people's ears sticking out of their heads. Over time, corn cobs came to be known as ears of corn.

**Q. Why does popcorn pop?**

**A.** Popcorn kernels are different from other corn kernels in that they have been partly dried and have a tough outer shell. When they are heated, the insides swell and press against the kernel's shell. When the insides are big enough, they break the shell and make a popping noise.

**Q. Why do potatoes have eyes?**

**A.** Potatoes don't have eyes like people do. If you look at a raw potato, you see places where the potato dimples in. There might be a little bump in a dimple. When people saw potatoes for the first time, they thought the dimples looked like little eyes. They are really places where a potato root can grow.

**Q. How are potato chips made?**

**A.** To make chips, potatoes are cut very thin. The slices are fried in hot oil and sprinkled with salt. Other flavors, like onion or cheese, might be added. Special chemicals called preservatives are also put in to keep the chips fresh in the package.

**Q. Are yams and sweet potatoes really potatoes?**

**A.** Potatoes, sweet potatoes, and yams all belong in separate plant families. The potato's cousins are red peppers, tomatoes, and eggplants. A sweet potato was called a potato because it looks like one. It is usually yellow or orange inside. It is drier than a yam and grows in many places. Yams can only be grown in countries with warm weather.

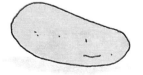
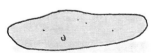

**Q. Why is soup called "soup"?**

**A.** A long time ago, people didn't use spoons or forks. This was before they were invented. Because they had no spoons, people would dunk chunks of bread into hot food to soak up tasty juices. The word for this kind of eating was *sop* or *sup*. You can see that the word *soup* was not far behind.

**Q. Why do people dress salads?**

**A.** When you put dressing on a salad, you are pouring a mixture of oil, vinegar, herbs, and spices on it. People like salad dressing because it puts interesting tastes on the vegetables in the salad.

**Q. Why do salads have lettuce in them?**

**A.** Green salads have lettuce. But other kinds of salads like macaroni salad, potato salad, and coleslaw (cabbage salad) may have no lettuce. In green salads, lettuce is the base. Whatever you add to it makes the salad your own. There are many kinds of lettuce you can choose. The most popular are light-green iceberg lettuce and dark-green Romaine lettuce.

**Q. Why are soda pops fizzy?**

**A.** Soda pops are made of carbonated water. This is water that has been shot with little air bubbles. Sugar and flavorings are added to make the different kinds of soda pop. Then it is quickly put in bottles and sealed. When you open a bottle or can, that whoosh you hear is bubbles escaping. If you leave the bottle open, the little bubbles will leak out and your soda pop will not have bubbles.

**Q. How can you drink food?**

**A.** You usually think of chewing when you imagine eating food. But food can be in the form of a drink. A milk shake and fruit juice are two kinds of liquid food. Many vegetables like tomatoes, celery, and carrots can also be made into juice. This is because most fruits and vegetables have a lot of water in them.

**Q. How can water be food?**

**A.** Everything you eat and drink has water in it. You probably never thought that the clear stuff we call water is food. Without water you would only live a few days. About half of your body is water.

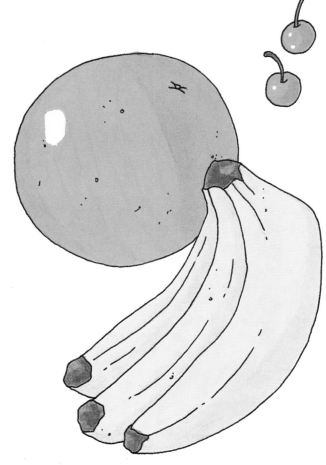

**Q. Why do people say "an apple a day helps keep the doctor away"?**

**A.** People have used this saying for a long time. They mean that apples have many things in them that are good for you. They are also a sweet treat in place of candy or cookies. If you eat things like apples, you'll be healthy. Then you won't see the doctor very often.

**Q. What are citrus fruits?**

**A.** Oranges, limes, lemons, and grapefruit are all citrus fruits. They come from trees that can only grow in warm places. Cold weather can kill an orange tree and make the insides of oranges dry and pulpy. In the United States, citrus fruits come from California, Arizona, Texas, and Florida.

**Q. What are the most popular fruits?**

**A.** The favorite fresh fruit in the United States is the banana. More apples and oranges are eaten, but usually in the form of juice or in other foods. Americans eat almost 19 pounds of bananas a year for every person. Bananas come from countries where the weather is warm. Almost no bananas are grown in the United States.

**Q. Why do many fruits taste sweet?**

**A.** Many fruits have a natural sugar in them called *fructose*. It is made by the plant when the fruit is growing. Natural sugar is better for your body than the sugar you get in candy because there isn't as much of it. And it's not ground up and cooked in a factory before it gets to you.

**Q. Why do people like sandwiches for lunch?**

**A.** Sandwiches are easy to carry and easy to eat. You don't need a knife, spoon, or fork. The bread holds everything you're eating. And the bread can be eaten too. Lunch is a good time to have sandwiches because there usually isn't much time to eat.

**Q. Why is a sandwich called a "sandwich"?**

**A.** John Montagu who lived in Sandwich, England, a couple of hundred years ago invented the sandwich. He didn't do much of anything well, but he did like to play cards. He never wanted to stop to eat. So he decided he could still eat and play if he put a piece of meat between two pieces of bread. Other people liked this new idea.

**Q. Why is ice cream sold in cones?**

**A.** You don't need a dish or a spoon to eat an ice cream cone. The cone is the dish and your tongue is the spoon. On a hot day at the St. Louis World's Fair in 1904, an ice cream seller ran out of dishes. A nearby waffle-maker heard the angry ice cream customers. He brought over rolled waffles. Ice cream was put in the waffles and the ice cream cone was born.

# BURGER TOWN

| | |
|---|---|
| HAMBURGER - 50¢ | FRENCH FRIES - 55¢ |
| SUPER HOT DOG - 60¢ | POTATO CHIPS - 35¢ |
| PIZZA PER SLICE - 60¢ | MILK SHAKES - 60¢ |
| SODA - 45¢ | CANDY - 35¢ |

**Q. Is there ham in hamburgers?**

**A.** The usual hamburger you get in a restaurant has no ham in it. Ham is pork, which is made from pigs. Burgers usually are beef, which is made from cows. Long ago, hamburger meat first came from a town in Germany called Hamburg. Hamburger was first served without the bun.

**Q. Why is a hot dog called a "hot dog"?**

**A.** A hot dog is really a sausage that was first called a frankfurter. Frankfurt is a German town where sausages like hot dogs were first made. When they first appeared in the United States, people were given white gloves to hold the franks with while eating them. Someone thought of using a bun when people didn't return the gloves. The name *hot dog* came from a cartoon about a dog that looked like a frankfurter.

**Q. Why do people call some foods "fast food"?**

**A.** Fast food is food you can buy and eat in a hurry. It's sold in restaurants that specialize in burgers, sodas, French fries, or pizza. These restaurants pride themselves on being able to fix you a meal within a few minutes after you order it. This service is handy for people who don't have much time to eat.

**Q. Is fast food the same as junk food?**

**A.** Not always. Many people think of junk food as food that doesn't give your body anything healthy to live on. These foods might be candy, chips, soda pop, gum, cakes, and Popsicles. These foods are fast. Just take off the wrapper and eat. Fast food restaurants do serve some things like soda pop and chips. But not all fast foods are junk foods. There are good things in hamburgers and pizza.

**Q. Where does chocolate come from?**

**A.** Chocolate comes from a cacao tree. This tree only grows in places that are hot year-round. Big pods grow out from the trunk. Inside the pods are seeds. These seeds are the cocoa beans from which chocolate is made. The beans are dried, then shipped to other countries. There they are made into chocolate foods.

**Q. Why is some chocolate marked "unsweetened"?**

**A.** The chocolate that you taste in candy and cakes is not the real taste of chocolate. That is chocolate with sugar added. Chocolate by itself has a bitter flavor. Long ago, when people first found out about chocolate, the favorite way to have it was in a hot drink. No sugar was added. People put vanilla or hot spices like pepper in it.

**Q. Why are some foods "artificially" flavored?**

**A.** All natural flavors come from plants. *Artificial* means "not real." Artificial flavors are made by chemists. They study the chemicals that are in the real flavor and try to copy them. Because artificial flavors can be made in large amounts, they are cheaper to use in food products than real flavors.

**Q. Where does salt come from?**

**A.** Salt is a mineral that comes from the earth. There is also a lot of it in the oceans. Long ago, salt was valuable. It was one of the few seasonings for making food taste better and for preserving meat. It was hard to get. Today people have better ways to get salt from the earth and sea. It can be bought anywhere.

**Q. Why are herbs and spices put in foods?**

**A.** Many people would agree that a lot of food dishes would not be so good to eat if it weren't for herbs and spices. They are used to flavor foods. You can take the same food, such as noodles, and give it many different flavors with different herbs and spices.

**Q. How are herbs and spices different?**

**A.** The leaves or stems of plants are used as herbs. Some kinds of herbs are basil, sage, rosemary, and mint. Spices come from other parts of plants, such as the flowers and seeds. Mustard and nutmeg come from seeds. Cloves come from flowers. Cinnamon comes from the inner bark of a tree. Ginger comes from a plant root.

## Q. Where do peanuts come from?

**A.** Peanuts are the pods of a bushy plant that grows underground. Peanuts aren't nuts at all. They are really a kind of pea and belong in the same food family as beans. Peanuts were first grown in South America long ago. In the United States, they were first grown in Virginia and North Carolina.

## Q. Why is peanut butter called "butter"?

**A.** Peanut butter spreads on bread a lot like soft butter. That's why it's called peanut butter. It doesn't really have butter in it. It may have salt and some sweetener. Since peanuts are oily, it may also have some hardened oil that keeps the peanuts from separating from the peanut oil.

## Q. What other foods are peanuts in besides peanut butter?

**A.** You'll find peanuts in salad oil, mayonnaise, margarine, cheese, flour, and candy. But you may have peanuts in your house in more places than you think. They are used in paints, wood stains, ink, and shaving cream. The shells are used in plastics and wallboard. The peanut is one of the most useful plants we have.

**Q. Why do doughnuts have holes?**

**A.** No one really knows. There are many stories. One says that a sea captain put a fried cake on one of the spokes of the ship's wheel when he needed both hands to steer. Bakers agree that doughnuts cook better with the hole. Without it, they say, the doughnut would be too doughy.

**Q. Why does spaghetti come in so many different shapes?**

**A.** Spaghetti is actually the name of only one kind of pasta. There are many different shapes—shells, short tubes, long strings, and little elbows. Each shape was invented in a different place. In Italy, where most pastas come from, different shapes are used in different dishes. Different shapes for food make eating more interesting.

**Q. Why aren't eggs round?**

**A.** Round eggs would roll out of the chicken's nest! Oval shaped eggs roll in a circle. This helps the egg stay in the nest until it is ready to hatch. The oval shape also makes the egg stronger. A round egg is more likely to crack.

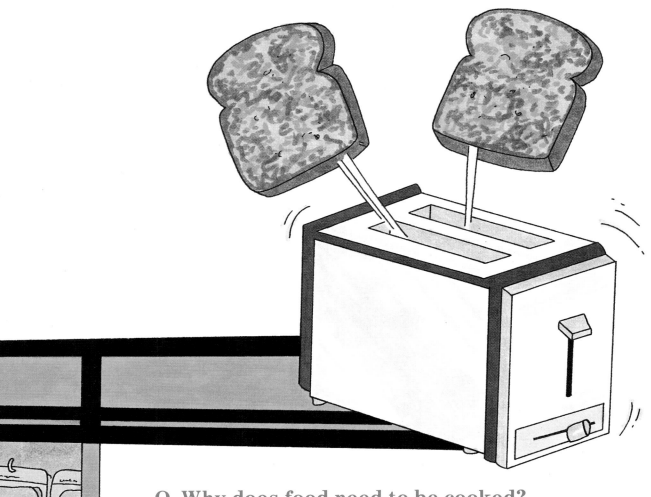

**Q. Why does food need to be cooked?**

**A.** You can eat some foods raw, or uncooked, like carrots and apples. Other foods, like meat, have to be cooked so they are safe to eat. If you ate them raw, you might get sick. Some foods like eggs just look and taste better if they're cooked. And other foods just aren't finished unless they're cooked. Look at a bowl of cake batter. It doesn't look much like a cake until it's baked.

**Q. Why do people measure things when they're cooking?**

**A.** Almost every recipe in a cookbook tells you how much of each thing to put in what you're making. You might put a cup of flour in pancakes, but only a teaspoon of salt. If you didn't measure things, your food might not taste good or look right when you're finished.

**Q. Why are there grocery stores as well as supermarkets?**

**A.** Any store you buy food in is a grocery store. *Grocery* is another word for food. A *market* is also a place to buy food. Grocery stores and markets can be small. A supermarket is big. It carries the greatest number of different kinds of food. People used to go to different stores to buy meat, fruits and vegetables, milk, and flour. When supermarkets were built, people could buy everything they needed in one place.

### Q. Why are raisins so wrinkled?

**A.** Raisins are really grapes that grow on grapevines. A lot of the raisins in this country come from California. After they are picked, the grapes that will become raisins are laid out in the sun. There they sit for almost 2 weeks until they are dried, wrinkled, and sweet. Then they are stored in big bins until they are ready to be put in boxes and sent to the stores.

### Q. What kind of vegetable is a pickle?

**A.** The most common kind of pickle is really a cucumber. The cucumbers are sliced and then soaked in vinegar. Then the pickles are flavored with different spices and tightly sealed in jars. Pickles can be sweet or sour. The most common sour pickle is the dill pickle. Other vegetables that can be pickled are tomatoes, beets, onions, and red and green peppers.

### Q. Why do jelly beans come in so many colors?

**A.** Jelly beans are not real beans. They are candy made of sugar and flavorings. Because jelly beans are made by people instead of grown on bushes or vines, they can be any color people decide to make them. They might make them red, blue, purple, pink, black, white, yellow, orange, or green. Each color has a different flavor.

**Q. Why do onions make you cry?**

**A.** The juice in onions has something in it that bothers people's eyes. When you cut an onion, the juice is released into the air and floats up to your eyes. When your eyes sense the onion juice, they try to get rid of it by crying. You can help this problem by rinsing the onion and the knife in cold water first.

**Q. What does it mean to have a food allergy?**

**A.** When your body reacts badly to something you feed it, you may have an allergy. You may itch, get a headache, or feel sick to your stomach. A lot of people have allergies to all the foods in one group: nuts, chocolate, or foods with milk in them. They have to remember not to eat these foods.

**Q. Are vitamins food?**

**A.** Vitamins are parts of food that your body needs. They are not food by themselves. Your body needs Vitamin A for strong eyes. It needs Vitamin B for a healthy brain. You usually get all the vitamins you need in the food you eat. If you don't, you should take a vitamin pill.

**Q. Why do we keep some foods in the refrigerator?**

**A.** Germs attack food very quickly in warm temperatures causing it to go bad. In the refrigerator, the cold air stops the germs, so that we can keep things fresh for a very long time. Certain foods taste a lot better when they're cold, don't you think?

# THINGS THAT GO

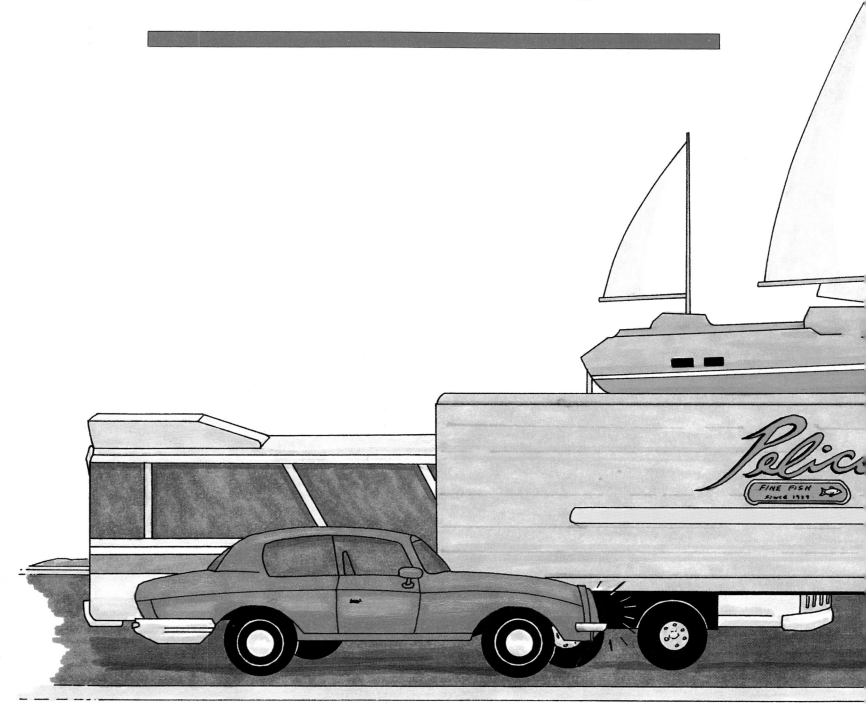

## Q. How does a hot-air balloon stay up?

A. A hot-air balloon is made of the same material used in parachutes. Gas from tanks is burned to make hot air so the balloon would fill up. Since hot air is lighter than cool air, it lifts the balloon up. As the air cools, the balloon comes down.

## Q. How do people steer hot-air balloons?

A. The only directions balloonists can control are up and down. Going forward or backward depends on the wind. People who travel in balloons must know a lot about the wind. They must know how high and how fast different layers of wind called *currents* blow.

## Q. Why are hot-air balloons so colorful?

A. Balloonists want people to see their balloons in the sky. So they make the balloons out of bright colors that show up against the blue sky. The balloons may have stripes, stars, circles, or pictures of animals on them. From the ground, you can pick your favorite balloon and watch as it floats by.

**Q. Why do helicopters fly straight up?**

**A.** Helicopters have a large propeller on top. When the propeller whirls around, it moves so quickly that it creates a strong wind. The wind moves down pushing the helicopter up. Once the helicopter is in the air, the wind caused by the propeller moves the helicopter through the air.

**Q. What can a helicopter do that an airplane can't do?**

**A.** A helicopter can go in almost any direction. It can fly straight up, backwards, and sideways. It can even stay in the air over one spot. This is called *hovering*. It can make sharper turns than airplanes can. It can land on the top of a building. And it doesn't need a long runway in order to take off.

**Q. What kind of work does a helicopter do?**

**A.** People use helicopters for many different jobs. They lift heavy things to the tops of buildings. They carry people to places that are hard to get to such as a hospital, a jungle, a mountaintop, an oil rig at sea, or the middle of a busy city. Some radio stations use helicopters to make traffic reports to tell listeners which roads are crowded.

**Q. How do people get fresh air high up in an airplane?**

**A.** Large passenger planes fly high above the earth where the air is thin and cold. A person could not live in it. So the plane has a way to bring the outside air into a part of the engine. Here the air is heated. Tanks store the air and pipes take this air to different parts of the airplane.

**Q. How does an airplane land?**

**A.** The pilot uses many instruments to find out how close the airplane is to the ground and to the airport. These instruments use radar to pick up radio signals from the ground. Lights in the airplane turn on when the airplane passes certain points on the ground and comes closer to the airport. Then the pilot knows where to go.

**Q. How does a heavy airplane get off the ground?**

**A.** An airplane is heavier than air. It can fly because the wings are a special shape. They have a flat bottom, a round front, and a curved top. They direct the air so that it lifts the plane. The faster the plane goes, the greater the lift. That is why an airplane must go fast down a runway to take off.

**Q. What happens to your suitcase when you check it at an airport?**

**A.** You leave your suitcase at the counter. From there it goes to a baggage room. The baggage workers read the tag to see which airplane the suitcase will travel on. They put the suitcase on a cart. The suitcases on the cart are loaded into the airplane. When you land, the baggage workers at that airport unload your suitcase.

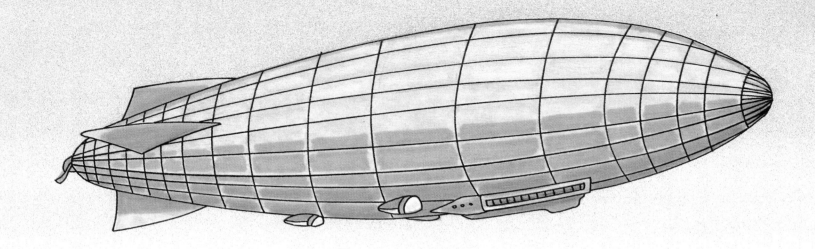

## Q. What are those big blimps you sometimes see in the sky?

A. The blimps that float over sports games and other big events are airships. They are like balloons filled with a lighter-than-air gas. Engines and propellers move the airships through the skies. To go up, heavy bags of water or sand are released. To come down, gas is let out of the airship.

## Q. How does a jet engine work?

A. A jet engine works a little like a balloon you blow up and then let go. If you haven't tied the end, the balloon flies all over. The air rushing from the inside to the outside pushes the balloon. A jet engine sucks in a large amount of air. Fuel is put into the air to make the air burn. The hot gases rush out of the tailpipe. This pushes the jet forward.

## Q. How fast can jets fly?

A. Air Force jets fly very fast. Many of them go about 2,000 miles per hour. Even sound travels much slower than that. Most airplanes people take usually fly about 600 miles per hour. They can go across the United States in about 5 hours. An Air Force jet that started at the same time would have landed 3 hours earlier.

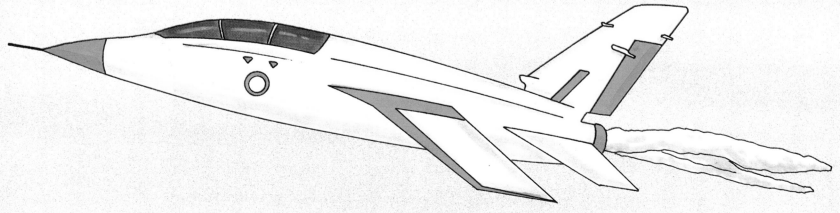

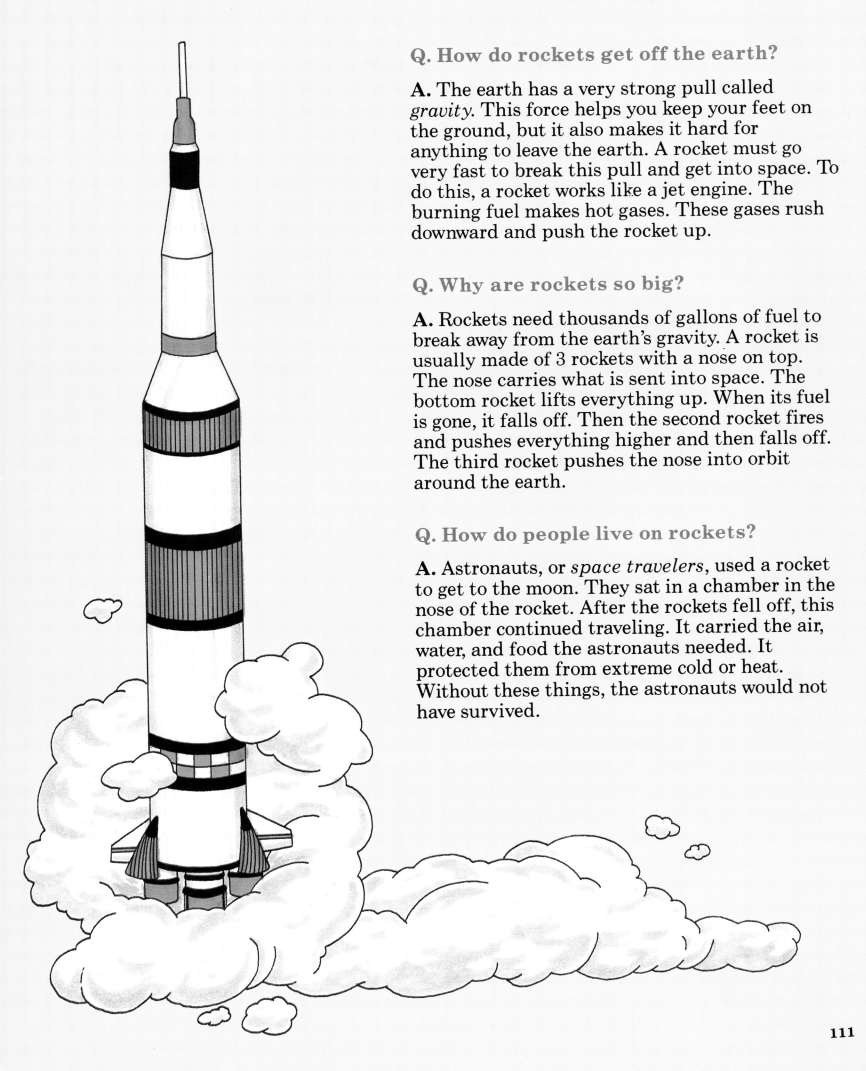

## Q. How do rockets get off the earth?

**A.** The earth has a very strong pull called *gravity*. This force helps you keep your feet on the ground, but it also makes it hard for anything to leave the earth. A rocket must go very fast to break this pull and get into space. To do this, a rocket works like a jet engine. The burning fuel makes hot gases. These gases rush downward and push the rocket up.

## Q. Why are rockets so big?

**A.** Rockets need thousands of gallons of fuel to break away from the earth's gravity. A rocket is usually made of 3 rockets with a nose on top. The nose carries what is sent into space. The bottom rocket lifts everything up. When its fuel is gone, it falls off. Then the second rocket fires and pushes everything higher and then falls off. The third rocket pushes the nose into orbit around the earth.

## Q. How do people live on rockets?

**A.** Astronauts, or *space travelers*, used a rocket to get to the moon. They sat in a chamber in the nose of the rocket. After the rockets fell off, this chamber continued traveling. It carried the air, water, and food the astronauts needed. It protected them from extreme cold or heat. Without these things, the astronauts would not have survived.

111

**Q. How does the space shuttle fly?**

**A.** A rocket takes the space shuttle into space by working like a jet engine. It burns gases to make fuel. When these gases get hot enough, they rush downward and push the rocket up. When the shuttle is ready to come back to the earth, the crew turns on the engines. This helps slow down the shuttle. Then they fly it back to the earth and land it like a glider.

**Q. What jobs does the space shuttle crew do?**

**A.** The shuttle crew takes satellites into space. They put these satellites into orbit around the earth. They have even fixed broken satellites that were already in space. The crew also takes pictures of the earth. They do science experiments to find out more about the sun and stars. They also study how well people can live in space.

**Q. What might the shuttle do in the future?**

**A.** People might some day live and work in outer space. The shuttle will help people build space stations where they can live. It will carry people and even building materials from the earth to the station. The things people make in space will travel back to the earth on the space shuttle.

TUGBOAT

**Q. What do tugboats do?**

**A.** Tugboats are used to move large ships. They pull or tow big ships into the harbor or they push the ships from the back. Then they help the big ships find their places at the docks.

**Q. What are some of the different kinds of tugboats?**

**A.** Besides the tugs that push and pull big ships, there are special "pusher" tugs. These tugboats pull and push flat barges on rivers and canals. Other tugs are made to go out into the sea to help damaged ships. Some tugs are fire fighters. They carry hoses and other equipment to fight fires on ships and docks.

**Q. What is a submersible?**

**A.** A submersible is a small or mini-submarine made to go deep into the ocean. It has windows so people can see out. It also has lights because the deep ocean is very dark. There are cameras to take pictures. There is even a 2-way radio to talk to the ships above.

**Q. What do people find with submersibles?**

**A.** Workers use submersibles to help them lay pipelines and to build oil rigs. Scientists use them to look for valuable minerals. One submersible named *Alvin* helped to find and explore a famous ship called the *Titanic*. The Titanic sank in 1912 when it hit an iceberg in the ocean.

SUBMERSIBLE

## Q. How do people see out of a submarine when it is underwater?

**A.** A *periscope* helps people see what is going on above water. A periscope is a long tube that can be raised or lowered or turned in any direction. It has mirrors on the top and bottom. The top mirror catches the view above the water. The bottom mirror shows a person in the submarine what the top mirror sees.

**Q. How does a submarine go up and down in the water?**

**A.** A submarine has special tanks just inside its skin, or *hull*. When the submarine is at the top of the water, the tanks are full of air. The light air floats the submarine. When the tanks are filled with water, the submarine sinks. Little wings on the side of the submarine move to help direct it. When the submarine is down far enough, a little air is put back into the tanks to stop the submarine.

**Q. How do people in a submarine know something is ahead in deep water?**

**A.** Often a submarine is too deep to use the periscope to see what is going on. Then an instrument called *radar* is used to find objects around the submarine. Radar uses electricity. It sends out radio waves like a flashlight sends out light. The waves bounce off objects—just like your voice bounces off a cliff—to make an echo. The radar listens for these echoes. They appear as little blips on a radar screen.

**Q. What is it like to be on a submarine?**

**A.** A submarine can seem cramped inside to someone who is used to big rooms. The hallways are narrow and the rooms are small. Every bit of space is used. There are no windows. A submarine may stay out in the ocean for many weeks. The people who work on the submarine must be used to working and living in small spaces.

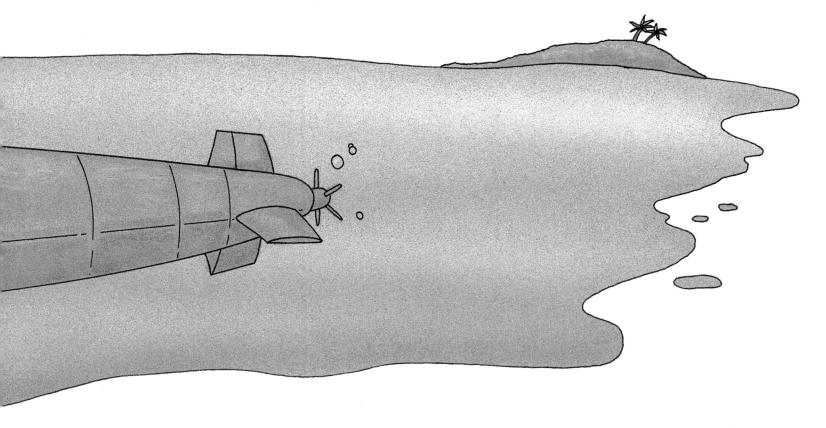

**Q. How does a boat's propeller make the boat go?**

**A.** A boat's propeller is made of flat blades on a long pipe. The blades are slanted so that they hit the water at different times. Each blade catches some water and pushes it back. The faster the propeller goes, the more water it pushes. This makes the water push the boat forward.

**Q. How do people drive boats safely with no traffic signals?**

**A.** There are no signs or traffic lights on a lake, river, or in the ocean. But there are rules. Anyone who wants to drive a boat must know these rules. Here are two rules for powerboats: When powerboats meet, they must signal with one horn blast. Then they pass to the left of each other. A boat that wants to pass a boat from behind must go to the right.

**Q. Why do boats need anchors?**

**A.** An anchor keeps a boat in one place. If you did not use an anchor, you might lose your boat when it drifts away. An anchor is also necessary to help steady a boat in bad weather. Anchors often look like big metal T's with the cross part of the T bent down. They are made this way so that the bent ends will dig into the ground underwater and hold the boat.

## Q. How does a sailboat go?

**A.** A sailboat uses the wind to push it across the water. It does this by catching the wind in fabric sails. The sails are made with curved edges. When the wind fills them, they look and act almost like airplane wings. The sails are attached to masts, which are poles that stand upright in the boat. The hardest part of sailing a boat is learning how to use the sails to ride with the wind.

## Q. What are some kinds of sailboats?

**A.** Sailboats can be small or large. There are small catboats that have one sail. A sloop has one sail in the middle and two other sails. There are many styles of catboats and sloops. The large sailboats are yawls, ketches, and schooners. These boats all have more than one sail and places for people to live.

## Q. Why do people like to sail?

**A.** Many people find it exciting to be in charge of a boat that is racing across the water with the wind. They enjoy the sun, the water, and the fresh breezes. They like learning what to do to sail the boat. They also enjoy being away from their everyday world.

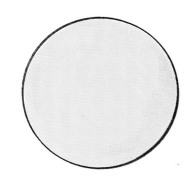

**Q. How do big cruise ships know which way to go in the ocean?**

**A.** When you are in the middle of the ocean, all you see is water. People who steer ships have charts and maps that show them the way the water flows. They also use instruments that tell them directions. One of these is a compass. Another is a sextant, which uses the stars to guide the ship.

**Q. Why do people like to travel on cruise ships?**

**A.** Some people believe that the best vacation is a trip on a ship. They enjoy being on the water. They also like the things they can do on a ship. They can go to a nice restaurant, go swimming, or play different outdoor games. They can even dance or go to an exercise class. Or they can just sit and watch the ocean. There are even things for kids to do.

**Q. What are some of the jobs people do on a big ship?**

**A.** A big vacation ship is like a floating town. Many people are needed to make it work. There are cooks in the kitchen. Stewards clean the passengers' rooms. A purser takes care of the money. A radio person talks to other ships and to the shore. The social director helps passengers find things to do. And, of course, there is the captain who makes sure everyone is doing a good job.

### Q. Why are canoes pointed at both ends?

**A.** Canoes are made to move through the water quickly and easily. The slim shape of a canoe and its pointed ends help make it fast and easy to steer. However, it also makes a canoe easy to tip over. Never stand up in a canoe. This makes the canoe unsteady. It can turn over and then everyone and everything in it will get wet.

### Q. Why does a canoe have to be paddled on both sides?

**A.** A canoe works best with two people paddling it. One sits in front and paddles on one side. The other sits in back and paddles on the other side. Then the canoe will go in a straight line. If there is only one person in a canoe, he or she must paddle first on one side and then on the other to keep the canoe straight.

### Q. How are a canoe and a kayak different?

**A.** A kayak is shaped like a canoe, but the ends do not curve upward. It has a top with a round hole where the rider sits. The hole is made small so no water gets into the boat. A person sits or kneels in a canoe, and sits with his or her legs out in a kayak. A kayak's oar has paddles on each end.  A canoe's oar has just one paddle.

**Q. What do the words, letters, and numbers on the front of the bus above the driver mean?**

**A.** The letters and numbers tell you what route the bus travels. The street name tells you the limit of the route. Most bus companies have maps that show you the routes and their numbers. If you see a town or city name, you know the bus travels to that town or city and back again.

**Q. Why are city taxis yellow?**

**A.** Yellow is an easy color to see on the street. It helps people find taxis. But not all city taxis are yellow. In some cities they are black. In other cities they are black and white. Many TV shows are set in cities that have yellow taxis. So many people think that all taxis are yellow.

**Q. How do taxi drivers know what to charge people?**

**A.** Most taxis have *meters*. These are little machines that count up how many miles have gone by and how many minutes have passed. The taxi driver resets the meter every time a new person hires the taxi. The amount of money the ride costs is shown on the meter as the taxi runs. At the end of the trip, the driver stops the meter. The passenger pays the amount shown.

**Q. How does pushing the gas pedal make a car go?**

**A.** When you push the pedal, gas and air go into one of the car's cylinders. A cylinder looks like a big can with a piece of metal at the bottom. It comes up and squeezes the air and gas to make a spark. The gas explodes and pushes the metal piece down. This moves another piece of metal and turns the pipe connected to the wheels. The wheels turn and the car starts moving.

**Q. Why do cars need oil?**

**A.** A car's engine has many moving parts. These parts get hot when the car is running. They also rub against each other and wear out quickly. Oil coats an engine and carries away dirt and bits of metal. It helps keep the engine clean and running smoothly.

**Q. Why do cars have seat belts?**

**A.** Seat belts are for passenger safety. If a car hits something, passengers are thrown forward. Seat belts keep them in their seats. Then they won't hit their heads on the front window or on the front part of a car.

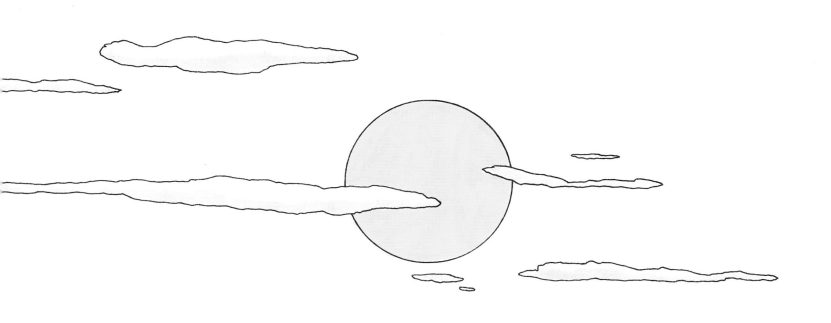

**Q. Why do ambulances have the word *ambulance* spelled backward on the front?**

**A.** Ambulances must get sick or injured people to a hospital quickly. To do so, they often must drive through city streets. All ambulances have a loud siren that tells people to get out of the way. But some people may not know the ambulance is right behind them. If they look in their rearview mirrors, they will see the word *ambulance* spelled correctly. In a mirror, letters reflect in the opposite order.

**Q. What do ambulances carry inside?**

**A.** Inside an ambulance you will see all kinds of equipment to help injured or sick people. There are oxygen tanks for people who have trouble breathing. There are bandages and medicines. There are stretchers to carry people on. There are machines to check a person's heart rate. The people who drive the ambulance are trained to use all of these things.

**Q. Why do people use tow trucks?**

**A.** Tow trucks take away cars and trucks that can't be driven and need to be moved. If a car breaks or becomes stuck, a tow truck moves it. If someone parks in the wrong place, a tow truck may take the car away. The tow truck backs up to a car. A big hook is put under the front or back of the car. The tow truck lifts the car and pulls it away.

**Q. Why are fire trucks red?**

**A.** Many people think of fire when they see red. So it makes sense for a red truck to fight fires. Then people know what kind of truck is zooming through the streets and why. Sometimes fire trucks are a lime green or yellow.

**Q. What does a fire truck carry?**

**A.** A fire truck carries the fire fighters. It also carries big, long hoses to spray water on a fire and an engine to pump the water. The truck also has axes that fire fighters use to knock down doors to get into a burning building. And it has a ladder that can go up high to rescue people from the windows of a burning building.

**Q. Where are fire trucks when they aren't fighting a fire?**

**A.** There are special buildings for fire trucks called fire stations or fire houses. The fire trucks are parked inside. There is also a place in the fire house for the fire fighters to eat and sleep while they are on duty. This way, they will be ready to go to a fire when the alarm sounds.

**Q. What do train whistles mean?**

**A.** Train whistles or horns are used to warn people and animals that a train is coming. They are usually blown at places where a road crosses the tracks. They are also used to signal the train crew or railroad workers. A signal might say that the engineer is going to use the brakes.

**Q. Why are freight trains so long?**

**A.** Freight trains carry a lot of things across the country. It is usually cheaper for businesses to send heavy things by train. So when a freight train travels, it pulls as many freight cars as it can. The length of a train also depends on what kind of freight it is pulling. Different kinds of freight need different kinds of freight cars.

**Q. What kind of freight cars do trains pull?**

**A.** Boxcars carry grains, cans, and packages. They look like closed boxes. Special refrigerated boxcars carry things such as fruit that would spoil if it got too hot. Flatcars are open platforms. They carry logs, steel, and machinery. Stock cars carry cattle, pigs, or sheep. Tank cars hold liquids such as oil.

**Q. What kinds of trains do people ride on?**

**A.** People travel on passenger trains. These trains carry people on short trips or on long trips that last many days. The trains that go on long trips are comfortable. They have bedrooms or staterooms where people can sleep. They have cars with seats for people to use during the day. They also have a dining car where people can eat at tables and look at the countryside going by.

**Q. Why are trucks called "semis"?**

**A.** The part of a large truck that pulls the load is called the tractor. The tractor pulls a trailer. A full trailer has wheels in the front and the back. A semitrailer doesn't have front wheels. The front is held up and attached to the back wheels of the tractor. Most drivers have shortened the name of this tractor-semitrailer to "semi."

**Q. Why do some trucks have so many license plates and numbers on them?**

**A.** Some truck drivers travel over many states to deliver loads. Each license plate shows that the truck can operate in that state. The numbers painted on the side of a truck show that the truck driver or the driver's company have paid money to the government so they can operate.

**Q. Where do truck drivers stay on long trips?**

**A.** Some drivers sleep in motels along the roads. Others may stay right in their truck if they have a cab behind the driver's seat. In this cab is a bed and places to store clothes and supplies. The driver can pull off the road, climb into the cab, and go to sleep. Special truck stops along the way give drivers a place to wash clothes and eat.

Q. Why are race cars so noisy?

A. Race cars have no muffler. A muffler looks a little like a partly flattened can. It goes under a car between the engine and the back pipe to help quiet the sound of the engine. But it also slows a car a little. Race car drivers don't want any extra weight on their cars. They don't want anything to keep the car from going as fast as possible.

Q. Why do race cars look so different from cars you see on the street?

A. Race cars are built for speed. They are low to the ground and have a thin, long shape. The faster a car goes, the harder it pushes against air. The air can slow the car down. A thin shape helps a race car slice through air so it can go faster.

Q. What happens when a race car takes time out from a race?

A. A race car runs at high speeds that quickly wear out tires and other parts of the car. At certain times, a race car has to pull into a place next to the track called *the pit*. Here a team of workers changes the oil, the tires, and anything else that wore out. They do their work in just a minute or 2.

**Q. Why do girls' and boys' bikes look different?**

**A.** Boys' bikes have a higher crossbar running from the handles to the seat than girls' bikes. Long ago, when people first started riding bikes, women rode in skirts. It was easier to get on and off a bike and to pedal it in a skirt if the crossbar was lower.

**Q. Why does the air go out of bicycle tires when the bike isn't used for a long time?**

**A.** There is a little valve on each bike tire where you put the air in. A little air always leaks from the valves. The tires' inner tubes are made of rubber. A small amount of air can leak through rubber too.

**Q. What does it mean when a bike has speeds?**

**A.** A bike with 3, 5, or 10 speeds has gear wheels of different sizes on the back wheel. By shifting gears on the handlebars, you move the chain from one gear wheel to another. On a flat or downhill road, you use a large gear that turns a small gear faster. Uphill, you switch to a fast, small gear that turns a large gear more slowly. The idea is to put more power in the bike without tiring yourself.

**Q. Why are there school buses?**

**A.** Some children live too far from school to walk. The way to school may also be across a dangerous, busy street. So a school bus picks up these children and takes them to school. This service started long ago when many people didn't have a way to take their children to school if they lived too far away.

**Q. Why are school buses yellow?**

**A.** Many public vehicles are yellow. Drivers learn that this color means to be careful around these trucks or buses. When a school bus stops, red lights flash. They tell other drivers to stop. The drivers must watch out for children going to and from the bus.

**Q. Why do school buses stop at railroad crossings?**

**A.** The law says that school buses must stop at railroad crossings. A school bus is large and cannot move quickly. A big train that is going fast cannot stop quickly. By stopping at the tracks, a school bus driver can look both ways and make sure there is no train in sight.

## Q. What is a snowmobile?

**A.** A snowmobile is like a motorcycle for riding in the snow. It runs on skis instead of wheels. Either 1 or 2 people can ride on a snowmobile. Supplies can also be carried on a snowmobile.

## Q. Why do people use snowmobiles?

**A.** In some parts of the country, there is a lot of snow in the winter. It is hard to keep the roads clear for cars. Some people even live in areas where there are no roads. Snowmobiles don't need roads. They are good for taking supplies to places that are snowed in. They are also used to rescue people in the snow.

## Q. What did people use before there were snowmobiles?

**A.** People who have always lived in snowy areas had ways to get around before snowmobiles were made. Eskimos used dog sleds. Supplies are strapped down on the sled and are pulled by several, specially trained dogs called huskies.

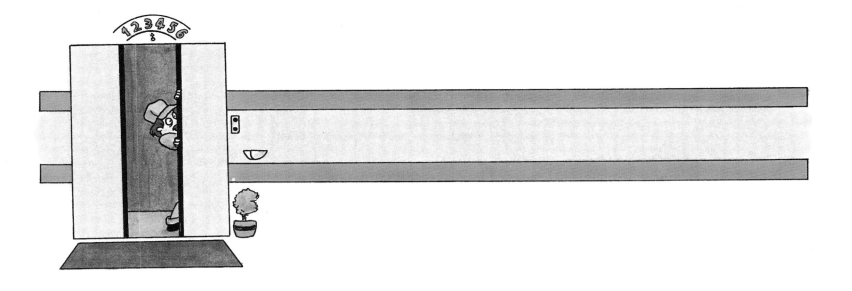

## Q. Where do escalator steps go in the floor?

**A.** The steps of an escalator form when they come out of the floor. The steps are really a big, motor-driven belt moving around on 2 rollers. Under the floor, the flat belt moves up as the steps above the floor move down. As the belt comes out of the floor, it gradually becomes steps. At the bottom, the steps flatten out again. This helps people get ready to step off.

## Q. How does an elevator work?

**A.** An elevator is like a big box. It is lifted up with strong steel ropes called *cables* that turn around a wheel driven by a motor. Every elevator has an emergency brake in case a cable breaks. An elevator won't work if there are too many people in it. It also won't move if the doors are not tightly closed.

## Q. How fast do elevators take you up?

**A.** When you travel up a tall building in an elevator, your body feels as though it is going very fast. But you are only going about 18 miles per hour. Steel cables hold the elevator on one end. A large weight is attached to the other end. As the elevator goes up, the weight goes down. This helps the elevator move up quickly.

**Q. Why are subways called subways?**

**A.** Subways are trains that move through tunnels under the earth. *Sub* means "under." And "way" is a route to travel. In some countries, a subway is called "the underground." Subways are only found in big cities. They are good ways to travel in places that have a lot of traffic on the streets.

**Q. How is a subway built under a city that is already there?**

**A.** Subway builders first make a map of where they want the subway to go. To go under streets, the workers tear up the road and dig a ditch. Then they cover the ditch so traffic can continue while they work. To go under buildings, the workers dig a hole that is deeper than the buildings' foundations. Then they build the tunnel underneath.

**Q. How do passengers breathe in subway tunnels?**

**A.** When a subway is built, special vents or airholes are put in the tunnels. These vents connect to the street above. Air comes into the tunnels through these vents. The subway cars also have special filters that the air goes through. This way some of the dirt from the tunnel is taken out of the air.

**Q. How do remote control toy cars go?**

**A.** *Remote* means "from far away." The toy cars you see zooming around by themselves are remote controlled. This means that the operator gives the car directions with buttons on a hand-held box. There are batteries in the car and in the box. Commands are sent through antennas on the box and on the car. One button may tell the car to turn. Another might tell the car to back up.

**Q. Why do kids like skateboards?**

**A.** A skateboard is a fun way for kids to travel. You can take it almost anywhere. It doesn't have to be parked like a bicycle does. You can carry it right into the house or a store. People enjoy watching a good skateboarder. You also get a lot of exercise using it.

**Q. How do kids learn how to do tricks on skateboards?**

**A.** Skateboard tricks take a lot of practice. A skateboarder needs good balance and strong legs. A safe place to practice is also needed. Serious skateboarders should always wear knee and elbow pads and a helmet. Learning to do tricks on a skateboard can lead to many falls at first.

# THE HUMAN BODY

**Q. Why do people learn?**

**A.** People can learn because they have a brain. Messages about new things go into the brain and are stored there. The brain is a little like a computer. As you see and do new things, the brain remembers them and saves this information so you can use it later on.

**Q. How much can people learn?**

**A.** The brain is an amazing thing. Even though it is not very large, it can store enormous amounts of information. People can learn just about anything they want to learn. Scientists say that people don't even use all of their brains. Imagine how smart you would be if you used your entire brain!

**Q. Does the brain control everything a person does?**

**A.** Yes. The brain is the part of the body that tells all of the other parts what to do. It does this by sending messages everywhere in your body. So when you stub your toe, your brain tells you that it hurts and that you should say "Ouch."

**Q. Why does your stomach sometimes hurt when you laugh too hard?**

**A.** When you laugh very hard, the muscles in your stomach and chest tense up. If you keep laughing, the muscles exercise really hard and may even start to hurt. But laughing really hard at something funny is much more fun than doing push-ups for exercise, don't you think?

**Q. Why do people smile when they are happy?**

**A.** Tiny babies can make their faces smile. When this happens, the grown-ups around them usually smile back and cuddle them. Because the baby likes to have loving people around, it soon learns to smile again and again. People continue this practice all of their lives.

**Q. Why do children play?**

**A.** Human children play more than any other kind of animal. Playing helps children learn and to practice things that grown-ups do. Playing also teaches children how to get along with one another.

**Q. Does everyone feel lonely at times?**

**A.** Everyone needs company at times. There are also times when everyone needs attention. It is not always possible to have company or get attention just when you want it. At times like these, a person feels lonely.

**Q. Why do people sleep?**

**A.** No one really knows why people sleep. One thing scientists do know is that people must sleep. Sleep is very important for a person's body. Without sleep, people become confused and cranky. Little children need a lot of sleep so that they have energy to learn and play all day.

**Q. What happens when a person sleeps?**

**A.** When you sleep, your body is taking a rest. Your body relaxes, and your heart beats more slowly. Your brain also takes a rest. The messages it sends to other parts of your body slow down. That is why when you sleep, you are usually not bothered by noises.

**Q. Why do people dream?**

**A.** No one knows for sure why people dream. Scientists are working to find the answer to this question. They do know that during a dream a person's mind wanders freely. This is very good because it lets people imagine doing things that they can not do when they are awake.

**Q. Why can people see?**

**A.** Our eyes are made of cells that gather light. When light touches these cells, they send a picture to the brain. The brain gets the information, and you can see.

**Q. Why do some people wear glasses?**

**A.** Some people have trouble seeing things that are far away. Others have trouble seeing things that are very close. This happens when light does not reach the right place in the eye. People wear glasses in order to correct any problems they have. Glasses help to bend the light so that it reaches the right place in the eye.

**Q. Why do we blink?**

**A.** Blinking helps to keep our eyes clean. We blink our eyes without even thinking about it. When our eyes close, a very thin layer of water covers them. Any tiny bits of dust that are on the eyes get washed away.

**Q. How do blind people dream?**

**A.** Blind people who once could see dream in "pictures" just as you do. People who were blind from birth dream in a different way. Their dreams have no pictures, but have lots of smells, tastes, touches, and even sounds.

**Q. Why can people hear?**

**A.** Ears help people hear. They are made in such a way that they gather sound. Sounds reach the ears and messages are sent to the brain. When the brain gets the messages, you can hear.

**Q. Why can some people wiggle their ears?**

**A.** Everyone has muscles in their ears. Most people cannot control these muscles, but some people can. When a person who can control these muscles makes them move, his or her ears wiggle.

**Q. Why do people's ears sometimes pop?**

**A.** When you travel in an airplane or in a tall building's elevator, sounds seem to fade away. Suddenly sounds come back and you hear a little pop. This happens because as you go up, the air around you is pressing on your ears. You hear a pop as your ears get used to the pressing air.

### Q. How long can hair grow?

**A.** Most people's hair never gets longer than 3 or 4 feet if they never cut it. This is because the individual hairs on your head grow for about 2 to 5 years before they fall out. But a man in India had hair that grew to be 26 feet long. That's a little longer than 4 tall men standing on each others' shoulders.

### Q. Why does hair turn gray as people get older?

**A.** The color of hair comes from a type of coloring called *melanin*. Hair is light or dark depending on how much melanin is in it. As people get older, the supply of melanin may stop. When there is no more coloring, the hair grows out gray or white.

### Q. Why do people have different color hair?

**A.** The color of hair depends on how much melanin is in it. Blonde-haired people have less melanin, even though they have more individual hairs. Black hair has more melanin, but people with black hair have about a quarter less hair than blonde-haired people. Red-haired people have the fewest hairs. What your hair color is also depends on what color hair your parents and grandparents have.

146

**Q. Why do some people have curly hair and others straight hair?**

**A.** What kind of hair you have depends on its shape. Straight hair is circular and curly hair is oval, or flat. The flatter the hair, the curlier it is and the easier it curls. Hair can change its shape depending on the weather. On a rainy day, your naturally straight hair may get a bit curly or your curly hair can get very curly. Whether you have straight hair or curly hair also depends on the kind of hair your parents and grandparents have.

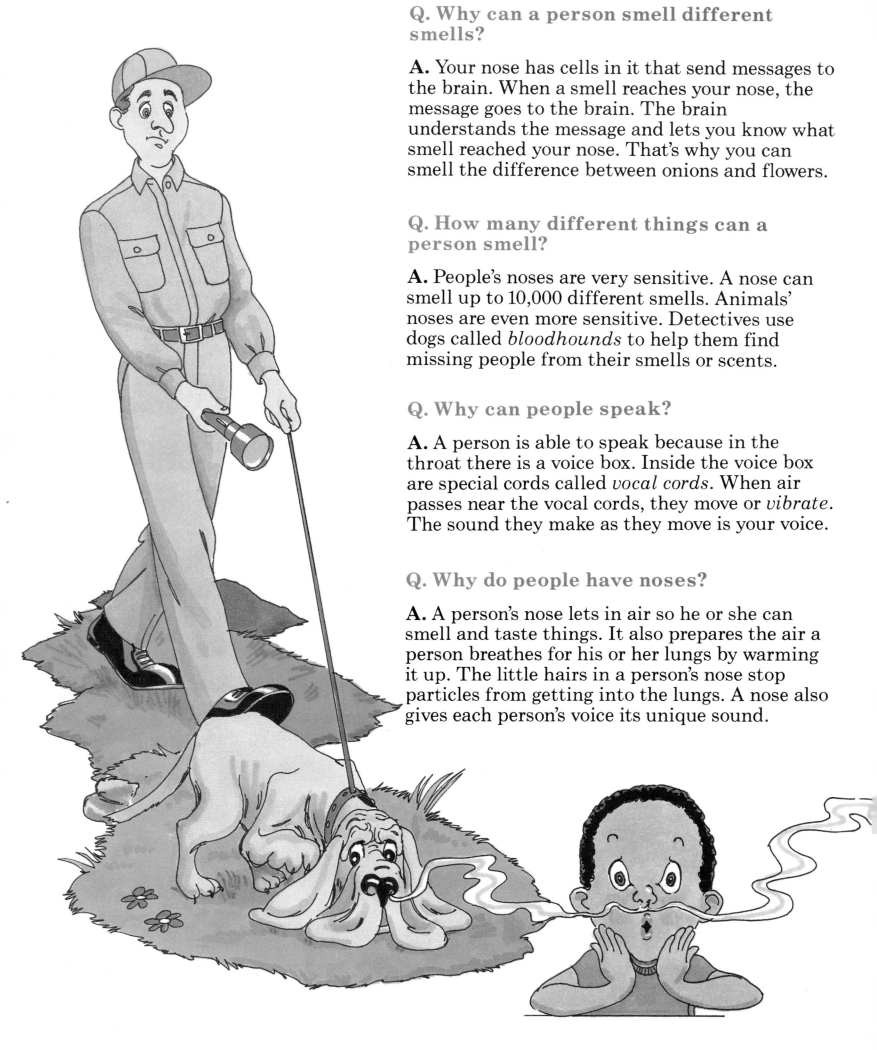

## Q. Why can a person smell different smells?

**A.** Your nose has cells in it that send messages to the brain. When a smell reaches your nose, the message goes to the brain. The brain understands the message and lets you know what smell reached your nose. That's why you can smell the difference between onions and flowers.

## Q. How many different things can a person smell?

**A.** People's noses are very sensitive. A nose can smell up to 10,000 different smells. Animals' noses are even more sensitive. Detectives use dogs called *bloodhounds* to help them find missing people from their smells or scents.

## Q. Why can people speak?

**A.** A person is able to speak because in the throat there is a voice box. Inside the voice box are special cords called *vocal cords*. When air passes near the vocal cords, they move or *vibrate*. The sound they make as they move is your voice.

## Q. Why do people have noses?

**A.** A person's nose lets in air so he or she can smell and taste things. It also prepares the air a person breathes for his or her lungs by warming it up. The little hairs in a person's nose stop particles from getting into the lungs. A nose also gives each person's voice its unique sound.

**Q. How do our bodies use food?**

**A.** After you swallow food, it goes into your stomach. It gets digested there, and tiny parts of the food are carried to all of the cells in the body. That is why people are concerned that you eat food that is good for you. They do not want unhealthy things traveling all over your body.

**Q. Why do people have spit in their mouths?**

**A.** People need spit in order to help them eat food. Spit helps you to swallow and helps break down foods that are difficult for the body to digest. It also keeps the throat slippery so that food can slide down to the stomach.

**Q. Does it matter how much you eat?**

**A.** If people do not eat enough food, their bodies won't have the energy they need to do all the things they want to do. If people eat too much food, not all of the energy will be used by the body. The energy that is left over is stored by the body and becomes fat.

**Q. Why is one foot usually bigger than the other?**

**A.** One foot is usually bigger than the other because we use one side of our bodies more than the other and have bigger muscles on that side of the body. This is not only true of our feet. Our entire body is not identical on the left and right sides. For most people the difference is very small. But there are people who have to buy different-sized shoes.

**Q. Why do people grow?**

**A.** A person's body is made of many different kinds of cells. As new cells are made, the body grows. When you are small, new cells are made very quickly, and you grow fast. As you get older, you grow more slowly.

**Q. Why do people stop growing?**

**A.** When people become adults, their bodies stop making new cells. When no new cells are made, the body stops growing. Everyone's body stops making new cells at somewhat different times. That's why some people are short and other people are tall. How tall you actually grow also depends on how tall your parents and grandparents are.

**Q. Is there really such a thing as a giant?**

**A.** Yes, there really are giants! The cells in some people's bodies never stop being made. And so they keep right on growing. There are some people who have grown to be over 8 feet tall! These people are called *giants.*

**Q. At what age do people grow the fastest?**

**A.** People grow most quickly in their first few weeks of life. Even before children are less than a year old, they are no longer growing as fast. Through childhood, children grow at a moderate rate. Girls start growing very fast again between the ages of 11 and 13; boys between the ages of 12 and 14. Then they slow down and grow very slowly until they stop growing altogether.

## Q. Why do people have tonsils?

A. Doctors think that people have tonsils to protect their throats from germs. Each person is born with 2 tonsils. There is 1 on each side of the back of the mouth.

## Q. Why do some people have their tonsils taken out?

A. Because the tonsils are at the top of the throat, they can collect germs. Sometimes tonsils get big and sore. When this happens, a person's throat hurts. If this happens too often, a doctor might operate to take the tonsils out.

## Q. How do germs get into the body?

A. If there is a cut or scratch on the skin, it is possible for germs to get into the body. Germs can also get in through the mouth or through any of the other openings in the body. If a person next to you has a cold and sneezes, you can catch his or her germs through your mouth and get a cold too.

## Q. What happens when germs get into the body?

A. There are cells in your body called *white blood cells* that are made to protect it. As soon as a germ arrives, these cells attack the germ and get rid of it so that you would not get sick.

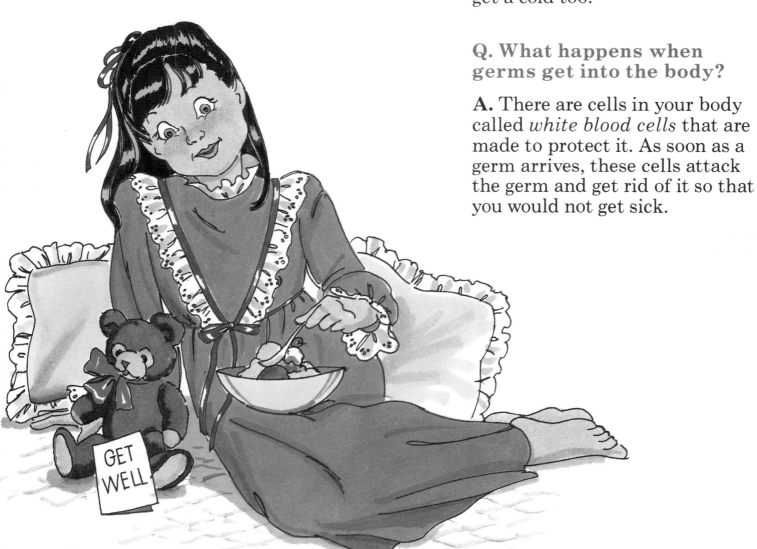

GET WELL

**Q. Why do people get fevers when they are sick?**

**A.** A fever is a rise in the body's temperature. That is why a fever is sometimes called a temperature. A higher temperature helps the body to fight off illness, since it makes it harder for germs to grow. A really high fever may even help you get rid of certain types of germs so that you can be healthy again.

**Q. What is a normal temperature?**

**A.** The temperature inside of your body is usually always the same. It is about 98.6°F. You can measure your temperature by putting a thermometer under your tongue. When your temperature is not normal, you should get plenty of rest so that you can get healthy very soon.

**Q. Why do people need to get shots?**

**A.** A shot, or a vaccination, keeps people from getting certain diseases. Little children usually get a lot of these shots, since their bodies need to become strong. Scientists and doctors have also developed many kinds of shots that make you well once you are sick. People get these kinds of shots all of their lives.

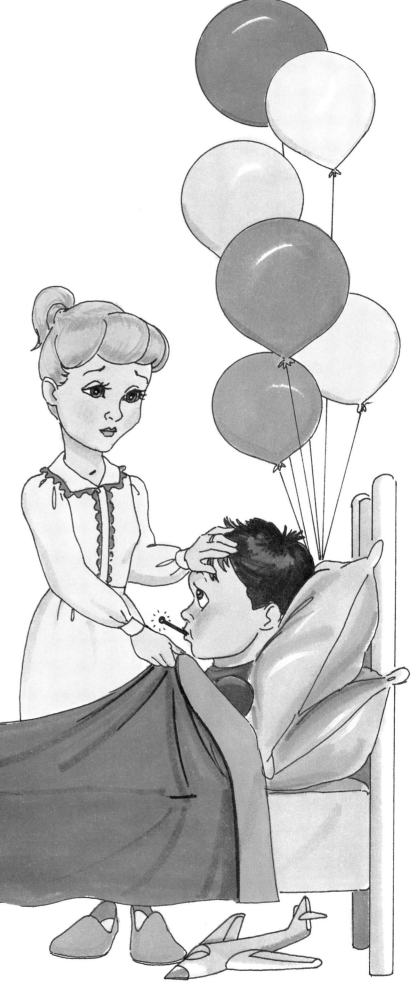

**Q. Why do people turn red when they are embarrassed?**

**A.** When a person is embarrassed, the brain automatically thinks that person is in danger. It sends a message that more blood is needed in the face muscles to help them fight off the danger. When this happens, you can actually see a little bit of the blood through the skin. Since blood is red, it causes the face to turn red.

**Q. What does the heart look like?**

**A.** When most people think of a heart, they think of the kind of heart that is on a valentine. Our hearts do not look like valentine hearts. They are about the same size and shape as a closed fist. A heart weighs just less than 1 pound.

**Q. What makes the heart beat?**

**A.** There is a special place inside the heart that keeps it beating. This spot in the heart gives off a tiny charge of electricity. This electrical charge makes the heart beat. It even knows how fast your heart should beat. If you are running, your heart beats a lot faster than if you are sleeping.

## Q. Why do people have muscles?

**A.** Muscles are the parts of your body that help it move. Your leg muscles help you to walk and run. The muscles in your chest help you to breathe. The heart is also a muscle. It pushes the blood to all the other parts of your body. Some people use certain muscles a lot and make them really big. Just compare the size of a football player's muscles to your own muscles.

## Q. How do muscles work?

**A.** There are different kinds of muscles in the body. Each kind is in charge of doing a certain thing, but all muscles work in the same way. The brain sends messages to the muscles telling them when to contract and when to relax. When you want to make a fist, the brain tells you to close your hand and contract your muscles. Then when you want to open your hand, you relax your muscles.

## Q. Will exercise make your muscles strong?

**A.** If you exercise, your muscles will stay healthy and strong. Before you begin to exercise, you should always slowly stretch your muscles to warm them up. A slow warm-up will keep you from hurting your muscles.

## Q. Why do people have bones?

**A.** All of the bones in a person's body make up the skeleton. Since bones are hard, they support and protect all of the inside parts of your body. Without the skeleton, people would have no shape to their bodies and would not be able to stand up.

## Q. What are bones made of?

**A.** Bones are made of a mineral called *calcium*. This mineral helps make bones strong. Inside of a bone is a soft material called *marrow*. The marrow inside of a bone helps to make new blood cells.

## Q. How does a broken bone heal?

**A.** As soon as a bone is broken it begins to heal. The brain sends messages to the bone to begin to make new bone cells. Shortly after the bone is broken, the body makes a layer of cells that protect the part of the bone that is broken. Of course, most people must wear a cast or a splint to keep the bone in the right position as it heals.

## Q. Are the bones in the body alive?

**A.** It may be hard to imagine a hard bone as being alive, but it is! There are cells inside the bone that are living and working. There are also tiny blood vessels inside of bones that bring oxygen and food to the bone cells.

**Q. What is a tickle?**

**A.** A tickle is a kind of feeling. One kind is when the skin is touched very lightly. The second kind is when certain parts of the body are pressed. You feel the tickle because of very sensitive nerves on your skin.

**Q. Why do people have a funny bone?**

**A.** People have a funny bone in their elbows. This is because a very large nerve in that area is only slightly protected from the outside. It is very sensitive. When you hit your elbow in that spot, you get a funny feeling in your arm.

**Q. Why do people have belly buttons?**

**A.** Your belly button is the place on your body where you were attached to your mother before you were born. After a baby is born, the cord that connects the baby to its mother is cut off. After the cord is cut, all that is left is the little scar called the belly button!

**Q. Why are some belly buttons "in" and others "out"?**

**A.** After the cord that connects a baby to its mother is cut, a small scab is formed. In a few days, this scab heals. Depending on how the scab heals, the belly button will be either "in" or "out."

**Q. Why do people have skin?**

**A.** Skin holds everything inside of your body together by acting as a kind of bag. It helps to protect the body from germs. Skin also helps the body to keep cool in summer and warm in winter.

**Q. Why are there so many different colors of skin?**

**A.** People all over the world have many different skin colors. It first depends on where people live. People with lighter skin usually live in cold places. People with darker skin usually live in warm places because dark skin helps to protect them from being burned by the sun. Materials called *pigments* give skin its color. The color of a person's skin also depends on what color his or her parents' skin is.

**Q. Why do older people sometimes get wrinkles?**

**A.** When a person is young, the skin cells in the body are smooth and a little rubbery. As a person gets older, the skin becomes drier and it loses its spring. When this happens, the skin droops into small lines and folds. These lines and folds are called wrinkles.

## Q. Why do people get hiccups?

**A.** People get hiccups when too much air gets into their lungs. The air hits the space around the lungs and moves the vocal cords. That is when a "hic" sound comes out. There really doesn't seem to be any useful reason for having the hiccups.

## Q. How can a person get rid of hiccups?

**A.** There are many things that people do to try to get rid of the hiccups. Some breathe slowly and deeply for 5 minutes. Others hold their breath as long as they can. Still others put a paper bag over their nose and mouth and breathe into it for a few minutes. Although there are many ways to try to get rid of hiccups, none of them is sure to work.

## Q. Why does the stomach growl?

**A.** The stomach is a very powerful muscle that is always working. It grinds food and pushes it where it can be used by the body. If you haven't eaten in a long while, there is only a little bit of food and some air left inside the stomach. When the stomach growls, you are really hearing the stomach grinding and mashing the leftover food and air. It is telling you that you should eat something soon.

## Q. Why do people get upset stomachs?

**A.** People get upset stomachs when they eat too much. They also can have their stomachs feel upset if they experience bumpy movements or spin around in a circle. Some people feel bad in cars or on roller coasters for this reason. Being upset or excited can also cause an upset stomach.

**Q. Why do people's noses run?**

**A.** People's noses run when they are cold or when they cry. When a person cries or when it is very cold outside, tears form in the eyes or in the nose. When tears fall from the nose, your nose is running.

**Q. Why do people sneeze?**

**A.** When something tickles the inside of your nose, you sneeze. The first part of a sneeze is when you take air in through your mouth. Some people say *aaaaaaaah* during this part of a sneeze. The *choooooo* part of the sneeze happens when the air comes rushing out.

**Q. Why do people burp?**

**A.** After you eat, the food in your stomach begins to get digested. As the stomach works on the food to break it into tiny bits, gases are given off. When the gases escape from the mouth, we call it a burp.

**Q. Why do people burp from drinking soda?**

**A.** The bubbles in soda are made of gas. When a person drinks soda, he or she is also drinking the gas bubbles. As the gas bubbles pop inside the stomach, the gas escapes from the mouth as a burp.

## Q. Why do people yawn?

**A.** When a person is sleepy or bored, there is not enough air reaching all of the cells in the body. The brain sends a message that causes the person to take a long, deep breath to bring more air into the body. This long, deep breath is a yawn.

## Q. Why do some people snore when they sleep?

**A.** Some people have a problem breathing through their noses. This might be caused by a cold or some other reason that makes a person's nose stuffed up. If people cannot breathe through their noses while they sleep and breathe through their mouths instead, very often you will hear them snore.

## Q. How does a person snore?

**A.** When a person is sleeping, the soft parts that can move inside the mouth and throat are relaxed. As air passes over them, they move around and bump and rub each other. This bumping and rubbing causes snoring.

**Q. Why do people's lips sometimes turn blue when they are cold?**

**A.** When a person is cold, the vessels that carry blood to all parts of the body tighten and there is less blood traveling. With less blood, the red blood cells in the lips lose some of their air and turn very dark red. When we look at the lips through the skin they look blue.

**Q. Why do some people have freckles?**

**A.** Freckles are small spots of color in the skin. Some people get freckles because their mothers or fathers have them. You can also get freckles if you spend a lot of time in the sun.

**Q. Why do people shiver?**

**A.** When people are cold, they need to warm up. Shivering is a movement that happens automatically. A person's muscles move back and forth very quickly and they produce heat that warms the body.

**Q. Why do people get goose bumps?**

**A.** People get goose bumps when they feel cold or frightened. When this happens, the tiny muscles in the skin around a strand of hair pull in. They form a tiny bump that we call a goose bump. Most often you will see goose bumps on a person's arms or legs.

## Q. Why do people cough?

**A.** People cough because something is tickling their throats. It might be a piece of dust or some food that got caught in a bad spot. People also cough when they have a cold. Sometimes people cough on purpose. They feel that something is in their throats and they want to get rid of it.

## Q. Why do people sweat?

**A.** People sweat to cool off when they are hot. When a person feels very hot, tiny drops of sweat form under the skin. As they come out onto the skin and dry, they cool you off.

## Q. Can you tell who is coughing by the sound of a cough?

**A.** It is easy to tell who is talking by the sound of a person's voice. But it is very hard to tell who is coughing from the sound of a cough. People with high voices sometimes have very low coughs. This is because the sound of a cough depends upon how much air blasts out.

**Q. Why do people have teeth?**

**A.** People need teeth in order to chew food. Think about how hard it would be to eat a carrot or chew a piece of meat without teeth! Teeth are the first step in helping the body to use food. Chewing helps to break food down into little pieces so that it can be swallowed and digested.

**Q. How do teeth grow?**

**A.** Teeth begin to form before a baby is born. They don't come up through the gums until a baby is about 3 months old. By the time a baby is about 2 years old, all 20 baby teeth have grown. When a child is about 5 years old, the baby teeth begin to fall out and are replaced by adult teeth.

**Q. Why do baby teeth fall out?**

**A.** Believe it or not, adult teeth are already in your mouth under your baby teeth, waiting to come out. When you are about 5 years old, the permanent teeth begin to push on the baby teeth. The baby teeth get loose, and begin to fall out.

**Q. Why do some children wear braces?**

**A.** Sometimes adult teeth do not grow in the right place in the mouth. When this happens, a child may have to go to a special dentist. The dentist will use braces to help to push the teeth into the right place in the mouth.

## Q. Why doesn't it hurt to cut your fingernails?

**A.** People feel pain when nerves in the body are hurt. Since the cells in fingernails are dead, there are no nerves in the nails. That is why is does not hurt to cut them.

## Q. What causes a black eye?

**A.** When someone is punched in the eye, tiny blood vessels under the skin get smashed. The skin around the eye usually turns purple since the blood escapes there. Soon the blood is broken down and the black eye turns green, yellow, and finally disappears just like any other bruise.

## Q. Why do people have eyebrows?

**A.** The hairs in an eyebrow are thick and stiff. These thick, stiff hairs trap bits of blowing dirt that might fall into the eyes. They also catch drops of sweat and keep them from falling into the eyes.

## Q. Why do people have eyelashes?

**A.** Eyelashes protect the eye. They are something like an insect's feelers. When they feel a speck of dust or a big wind they signal the brain. The brain sends back a message and the eyes close. There are about 200 eyelashes on each eye. They fall out and grow back all the time.

**Q. Why do people get bruises?**

**A.** People get bruises when they hit themselves hard and a little blood escapes under the skin. First the bruise looks like a red mark on the spot that you hit yourself. Then it turns dark blue and hurts when you touch it.

**Q. Why are bruises sometimes dark blue, green, or yellow?**

**A.** When you are bruised, the body goes to work repairing itself. The blood that has escaped under the skin is broken down and used again to heal the spot where you hurt yourself. As the blood works to heal that area, it changes from dark blue to green to yellow.

**Q. Why do people get scabs?**

**A.** A scab is a patch of crusty material that forms over a cut or scratch that has been bleeding. A scab is really dried blood and it forms to protect the wound from germs while it is healing. Once the area is healed, the scab falls off.

## Q. How much do newborn babies sleep?

**A.** Newborn babies sleep almost all of the time. This can be between 18 and 20 hours each day. They usually wake up every few hours when they are hungry. Sleep is very good for small babies because it gives them energy to grow and to learn about the world around them.

## Q. What is the first thing a newborn baby does?

**A.** The very first thing a newborn baby must do is breathe. Since it was not breathing on its own when it was inside of its mother, it must take its first breath as soon as it is born. The doctor usually taps the baby very gently on its bottom to make it cry. As soon as a baby starts to cry it also begins to breathe on its own.

## Q. Can newborn babies see?

**A.** Newborn babies cannot see well at first. It takes a while for their eyes to be able to focus clearly. But newborn babies can tell the difference between light and darkness.

## Q. How many babies can be born at one time?

**A.** Most of the time a mother has 1 baby at a time. Sometimes *twins*, or 2 babies, are born. Three babies, or *triplets*, and even 4, *quadruplets*, can be born. When this happens, all of the babies are born within a very short time. More than 4 babies can be born, but this is very rare.

**Q. Why are there twins?**

**A.** Each baby grows from 1 cell. Sometimes the cell splits in 2. When this happens, 2 babies grow. Sometimes, 2 cells begin to grow. When this happens, 2 babies will also be born. Two babies growing at one time are called *twins*.

**Q. Do all twins look alike?**

**A.** Twins that come from 1 cell that splits will look alike. These twins are called *identical* twins. Twins that come from 2 different cells will not look alike. These types of twins are called *fraternal* twins. There are more twins that do not look alike.

**Q. Can a boy and a girl who are twins look alike?**

**A.** Twins that look alike are always either 2 boys or two girls. A boy and a girl who are twins may look a little like each other, but they will not look exactly the same.

# EVERY DAY PEOPLE & THINGS

**Q. Why do people wear clothes?**

**A.** People wear clothes for protection. In the winter, clothes protect you from the cold. Boots and raincoats keep you from getting wet in the rain. And shoes protect your feet from pebbles, hot sidewalks, and icy streets.

**Q. Why are there uniforms?**

**A.** Uniforms help to tell us what people do. You know you are talking to a police officer from the blue uniform that she or he is wearing. Uniforms make people easier to recognize. It also makes the people who wear them feel like part of a team.

**Q. Do children wear uniforms?**

**A.** Many children who go to private schools wear uniforms to school. If you are a Brownie or a Cub Scout, you wear a special uniform to your scout meetings. Uniforms can make children feel very special—like they are part of a group.

**Q. Why are there police officers?**

**A.** Police officers keep neighborhoods running well. They help people and make sure that laws are followed. Police officers arrest people who have done something wrong to make sure that everyone in the neighborhood is safe.

**Q. Why do police officers wear badges?**

**A.** All police officers wear badges. It means that a police officer has finished police school and knows all the laws. Every badge has a number on it. When police officers write reports about things that happened, they use their badge numbers to tell who they are.

**Q. Why do people go to the doctor if they are not sick?**

**A.** In order for people to take good care of their bodies, they visit the doctor to get a checkup. This way the doctor can be sure that they are completely well. The doctor may also want to keep a patient up to date on vaccinations.

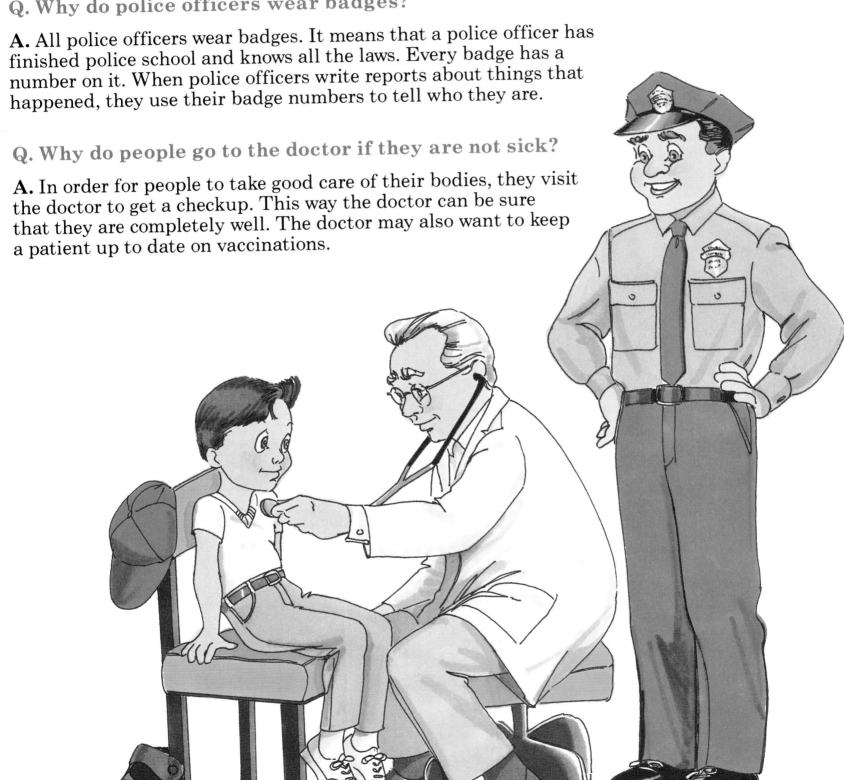

**Q. Why do people use library cards?**

**A.** Your library card allows you to take out books, records, videotapes, cassettes, and other things from the library. Your library card has your name and address on it. This helps the library keep track of who has borrowed what.

**Q. How can a librarian help you?**

**A.** Librarians are always ready to answer any questions you may have while you are at the library. They can help you find the things you are looking for or they can suggest books that you might like to read.

**Q. What happens if a person who wants to use the library does not have a library nearby?**

**A.** Sometimes people cannot get to a library, so the library delivers books to them. In some places there are special libraries on wheels. These are called bookmobiles. They visit people who don't have a library nearby.

**Q. What is the biggest library in the United States?**

**A.** The biggest library in the country is called the Library of Congress. It is in Washington, D.C. Just about every book that is published in the United States is kept in this library. You can imagine how many books it has—millions and millions!

**Q. How do teachers know what to teach?**

**A.** Most teachers follow a special plan that the school has prepared for each subject. They teach children how to read, write, work with numbers, and many other things. They learned how to teach these things by going to school themselves.

**Q. Where did television come from?**

**A.** The very first television was made in 1929 by a man named V.K. Zworykin. When television was new, there were only about 150 TV sets in America. Today, just about everyone has a TV. Some people even have more than one TV in their homes.

**Q. Were the first TVs like the ones we have today?**

**A.** The first TVs were very different from the ones we use today. They were very small and showed only black and white pictures. Usually the sound and the picture were not very good.

**Q. Do people ever watch TV for other reasons than for fun?**

**A.** Yes. TVs are used in many other ways. Sometimes, teachers use TV to help them teach students. Special TVs show people what is happening in faraway places. For example, special TV cameras can search the ocean floor for old shipwrecks! TVs can also be sent into space to send back pictures to scientists.

**Q. Why do you need to put a stamp on a letter?**

**A.** It costs the post office money to deliver your mail. A way that you help the post office pay for mail service is by putting a stamp on your letters. Without a stamp, your letter will be not be delivered.

**Q. Does everyone have mail carriers?**

**A.** If you live in a big city or town, you probably think that all mail is delivered by mail carriers. But this is not the case. In certain areas of the world, mail carriers use cars, trucks, bicycles, or even boats to deliver mail. Some people do not have any mail delivery—they have to go to the post office to pick up their mail themselves.

**Q. What is the busiest day of the year for the post office?**

**A.** If you think that mail is heaviest on Christmas, you are wrong. Valentine's Day is the busiest day of the year for a mail carrier. People send their Christmas mail early, but they want their valentines to arrive on Valentine's Day.

## Q. Why do knives that we use to cut our food have round ends?

**A.** People first started using knives as a weapon for fighting and hunting. When people began using knives at meals, they could not get out of the habit of fighting. One king in France got very angry and ruled that all table knives should have round ends so that no one could fight.

## Q. Did people always use forks?

**A.** Years ago, only rich people used forks. They did not want their sleeves to get dirty when they ate with their hands. Soon, the custom spread to everyone. The invention of the fork also ended the necessity of washing our hands during the meal.

## Q. When does the toast know it's time to pop out of the toaster?

**A.** Inside a toaster is a little clock called a *timer*. When you push the knob on the toaster to go down, the timer gets wound up. When the timer is all unwound, the spring makes your toast pop up.

## Q. How do keys work?

**A.** Most locks have 5 little rods called *tumblers*. They dig into the part of the lock that turns and jam it so that it can't turn. If you have the right key, the grooves on the key push the tumblers out of the way and let you unlock a door. They will never let you unlock a lock if you use the wrong key.

**Q. How did people tell time before there were clocks?**

**A.** People have been telling time for many hundreds of years. At first, people used the sun to help them tell time. They measured how long shadows were to tell what time is was. Through the years, different instruments such as hourglasses and sundials were also used to tell time.

**Q. How does a clock work?**

**A.** Some clocks must be wound in order to make them work. These clocks have a spring inside them that makes the clock's hands turn. Other clocks have pendulums. Pendulums swing back and forth to make the clock hands turn. Some clocks are electric. They have small motors inside them that make the hands turn.

**Q. Why are there zippers?**

**A.** Zippers are an easy way to fasten things together. They are used in many kinds of things. Zippers became popular in the early 1900s. They saved many people the time and trouble it took to lace up boots, button coats, and hook up the backs of shirts and blouses.

**Q. How do zippers work?**

**A.** Zippers have lines of tiny teeth along each side. When the sliding part of the zipper is pulled up, it pushes the teeth of the zipper together. When it is pulled down, the teeth come apart and the zipper opens.

## Q. Where did the idea of taking a bath come from?

**A.** Long ago, the ancient Romans built very large baths. Many people could bathe at one time. Later, people used big wooden tubs. They had to fill these tubs by boiling water and pouring it in. It took such a long time to fill these tubs that people did not take baths very often.

## Q. Did people always use a toothbrush to clean their teeth?

**A.** No, not exactly. Long ago, people cleaned their teeth by chewing on small sticks. Later, they used salt to make their teeth clean. Finally, people started using toothbrushes. Did you know that at one time toothbrushes were very expensive—they were made of gold and had jewels in them.

## Q. Where did soap come from?

**A.** It might be hard for you to believe, but long ago people used fat to clean themselves. They covered their bodies and hair with it and then put water on themselves when they wanted to clean off. They noticed that water, when mixed with fat, would clean the dirt and grease off of their skin and hair. To this day, soap is made from a kind of fat.

**Q. Where do puppets come from?**

**A.** Puppets have been a popular form of entertainment for a very long time. They were first used to tell legends and folktales. Usually they are a way to tell a story. Puppet characters are different from people. They can look funny and talk strangely—even animals talk when they are puppets.

**Q. How many kinds of puppets are there?**

**A.** There are many different kinds of puppets. There are puppets that fit over the hand. Some puppets are attached to a stick. There are even big puppets made of wood. When strings attached to their hands and feet are pulled, these puppets can move almost like people.

**Q. Where did music come from?**

**A.** Music has been around ever since there have been people in the world. Early music was very different from the music we listen to today. It often consisted of sighs, moans, shouts, dancing, clapping, and drumming.

**Q. What was the first musical instrument?**

**A.** The first musical instrument was the drum. It was first used to call together the members of a tribe. It was also used to drive away evil spirits. Since primitive people danced for all sorts of reasons, the drum was used to accompany the dancers.

183

**Q. Why are there rings in the circus?**

**A.** It is easier for the audience to see the show when circus performers work in a ring. The people are sitting all around the performers. This way they can see that everything that is happening is real and sometimes very dangerous.

**Q. Why are there clowns in a circus?**

**A.** Most of the acts in a circus are very thrilling. The audience watches daring trapeze performers, wild animal trainers, and acrobats who do dangerous things. Clowns entertain the audience in between all of the exciting and dangerous acts. They make people laugh and forget about the danger for a few minutes.

**Q. Why do tightrope walkers sometimes carry long poles?**

**A.** When tightrope walkers walk carefully along the rope, they must keep their balance so they will not fall down. Some tightrope walkers carry long poles to help them keep this balance.

**Q. Why do people jump rope?**

**A.** People jump rope for fun and exercise. Children have been jumping rope for many hundreds of years. They sing songs, jump rope, and have lots of fun. Other people like athletes jump rope to warm up their muscles before exercise.

**Q. Did children always have toys?**

**A.** We know that toys are very old because scientists have found them in the ruins of ancient cities. Children of ancient times played with dolls, wagons, rattles, toy boats, balls, board games, and many other things that children like today.

**Q. How are toys made?**

**A.** When someone invents a new toy, they sell the toy to a factory. People in the factory copy the toy and make many more just like it. In this way, children all over can enjoy the same toys.

**Q. Why do people play tricks on April Fools' Day?**

**A.** No one really knows how April Fools' Day got started. But most countries around the world have one day when people play tricks on each other. In the United States, that day is April 1. We call it April Fools' Day.

**Q. Why do people send valentines to each other?**

**A.** On February 14, people in the United States send valentines to their sweethearts as well as to their friends and families to show their affection. People started sending love letters and pictures on this date hundreds of years ago.

**Q. Why do we celebrate Mother's Day and Father's Day?**

**A.** The second Sunday in May is always Mother's Day. We celebrate this day to give special thanks to our mothers. The third Sunday each June is Father's Day. On this day we give special thanks to our fathers. Some people give their parents gifts on these special days.

**Q. Why do people eat turkey on Thanksgiving?**

**A.** People eat turkey on Thanksgiving to remind them of the Pilgrims. The Pilgrims came to America in 1620. Their first winter in the new land was very hard and they did not have enough food. But the Indians showed them how to grow crops and how to hunt. When the next fall came, the Pilgrims were sure they would have enough food to last the winter. So, they celebrated with a big feast that included turkey.

**Q. Why do people celebrate their birthdays?**

**A.** The custom of celebrating birthdays started many hundreds of years ago when the birthdays of important people were holidays. Soon everyone wanted to celebrate his or her birthday. Today, it is very common in the United States to have a birthday cake and to blow out the candles on it with one breath.

**Q. Why do people sing "Happy Birthday to You"?**

**A.** The song "Happy Birthday to You" is sung more times during the year than any other song in the world! It was written in New York in the 1930s by a schoolteacher named Patty Smith Hill. She loved young children and wrote the song for them to sing at birthday parties.

**Q. Can people have fun indoors?**

**A.** Of course! There are many ways to have fun indoors. Some people like to paint, draw, or do other kinds of art work. Others like to watch television, or play games. Many people enjoy reading books, magazines, or newspapers at home. Some people even like to cook.

**Q. How is paper made today?**

**A.** Today paper is made from wood, water, and chemicals. They are mixed together and put in a machine that stretches and presses it all into one big sheet. After all of the water dries out, the paper is polished so that it will have a smooth, level finish.

**Q. Why can pencils write?**

**A.** It is what's inside a pencil that makes it write. Many people think the dark part inside a pencil is lead. This is not true—the dark part of a pencil is called *graphite*. It leaves a black mark whenever you draw or write with it.

**Q. What is the alphabet?**

**A.** The alphabet is the 26 letters that we use to write any word that we can think of. The alphabet is sometimes called the ABCs. These letters came to us from the ancient Romans. There are many different alphabets in the world.

**Q. Why do people kiss?**

**A.** People kiss in order to show affection for one another. When we kiss someone on the lips, it means that we love them very much. A kiss on the cheek is a friendly and polite form of greeting. In some parts of the world, younger people even kiss the hands of their elders to show respect.

**Q. Why do we shake hands with our right hands?**

**A.** Long ago, men used to carry weapons in their right hands. When they wanted to greet a friend, they dropped the weapon and extended their empty hand. It was meant as a sign of peace and we use this custom to this day.

**Q. What is a wedding?**

**A.** A wedding is a ceremony at which two people get married. A couple gets married because they love one another and want to spend their lives together. A wedding can be in a church, in a synagogue, at the town hall, or even at home. Often, there is a big party after the ceremony to celebrate the couple's marriage.

**Q. Why do we throw rice at the bride and groom at weddings?**

**A.** Throwing rice at the bride and groom at weddings is an old tradition. Years ago, it was done to make sure evil spirits stayed away from the couple. Today, we throw rice to wish the newlyweds good luck and many children.

**Q. Why do people work?**

**A.** People work in order to earn money. They use the money they earn to buy things for themselves and their families. People also work because they like their jobs.

**Q. When do people work?**

**A.** Most people work 5 days a week on Monday, Tuesday, Wednesday, Thursday, and Friday. But some people also work on Saturday and Sunday. People who work on weekends usually take time off during the week.

**Q. Where do people work?**

**A.** There are many different kinds of jobs. Some people work indoors in stores or offices. Some people work outdoors. Airline pilots work up in the sky. People who work in the subway work underground. Do you know where your mother or father works?

**Q. Do children work?**

**A.** Sometimes children help their parents by doing jobs at home. They may wash dishes, make the beds, mow the lawn, or feed their pets. Some children help their parents plant crops, weave, cook, and other practical things.